SAN MIGUEL de ALLENDE:
A PLACE IN THE HEART

SAN MIGUEL de ALLENDE:

A PLACE IN THE HEART

Second Edition

Expatriates Find Themselves Living in Mexico

by

JOHN SCHERBER

SAN MIGUEL ALLENDE BOOKS

San Miguel Allende Books
Laredo, Texas

ACKNOWLEDGMENTS

Any book starts as an idea and by its completion becomes a joint effort.

Thanks to all those residents of San Miguel who shared their time and thoughts with me.

Thanks to my wife, Kristine, without whose support and suggestions this book would not be what it is.

Thanks to the late Wayne Greenhaw for a foreword that reflected his own long experience and unique perspective of San Miguel.

Thanks to my readers: Patti Beaudry, Bill Dorn, and Donna Krueger.

Thanks to Susan Page, tireless advocate for good writing, for her help, participation, and encouragement.

Thanks to Gerry Camp for editing.

Cover painting: Early Morning, Ten Ten Pie, by Tom Dickson

Cover Design by Lander Rodriguez

Author Photo by Gail Yates Tobey

Web Page Design by Julio Mendez

Second edition.

978-0-9832582-3-0

San Miguel Allende Books

Laredo, TX

www.SanMiguelAllendeBooks.com

ALSO BY JOHN SCHERBER

FICTION

(The Murder In Mexico Series)

Twenty Centavos
The Fifth Codex
Brushwork
Daddy's Girl
Strike Zone
Vanishing Act
Jack and Jill

(The Townshend Vampire Trilogy)

And Dark My Desire
And Darker My Wrath

The Devil's Workshop

To the expatriates of San Miguel

Table of Contents

FOREWORD

For an old hand who first came to the highlands of central Mexico more than fifty years ago, John Scherber's *San Miguel de Allende: A Place in the Heart* is entertaining, enlightening, and informative. Like the legendary Studs Terkel, he lets his subjects speak for themselves and adds reflections where needed.

In 1955, when I was fifteen, confined to a body cast in a Birmingham, Alabama, hospital, I'd undergone surgeries to correct scoliosis as a result of infant polio. In the children's clinic, fellow patients brought contraband literature. Among these was a men's magazine called *Saga* featuring an article, "How to Live in Paradise on $100 a Month," by a former GI living in San Miguel de Allende. I was fascinated, particularly with the photo of an artist sketching a nude model in a colonial courtyard. By now, I had already decided to be a writer.

In the summer of 1958, after finishing high school, I boarded a train and headed southwest. Four trains and six days later, I arrived at the depot where a rickety old taxi brought me into town. I gazed out the dusty windows at the pink spires of *La Parroquia Iglesia* and the other towers on the hillside. After checking in with the family where I would stay, I hiked down the hill to the Instituto to meet my creative writing professor, Ashmead Scott, and the director of the school, Stirling Dickinson. Stirling was a Midwesterner who'd been in San Miguel since the 30s, Scotty a veteran radio writer with vast experience in drama and humor.

That afternoon I ventured up to the *jardin* to La Cucaracha cantina under the western *portales,* just as described in the article. I met some of the tough old GIs who'd come to study art or writing. They mostly just sat and drank and told war stories. Their godfather was Chucho Chorea, the rotund proprietor who looked after the misbegotten souls of the Cuc. Not only was I eighteen, I was straight out of backwoods down-home Alabama, wide-eyed and full of innocent wonder.

San Miguel was a small town. With a population of less than 9,000 and fewer than 100 expatriates, its growth did not expand beyond *El Centro*. You could count the cars on two hands. On Sunday evenings at twilight, *mariachis* played in the bandstand and boys and girls walked in a promenade around the *jardin*, boys going one way, girls the opposite, with mothers and aunts watching every move.

Although I was enchanted, I soon grew homesick. Although the environment was mostly pleasant, it was not always. As you walked the streets, occasionally the whiff of sewage flowing beneath open grates hit the nostrils a hard blow. At night I listened to morose and mundane stories from the GIs. I drank too much, trying to keep up with the older guys and trying to disguise my obvious naiveté.

Leaving, every mile of track called out, "You gotta go back! You gotta go back!" At the University of Alabama I thought constantly about the town and talked about it and its people to my bored classmates. The next summer I came back. Again, I studied at the Instituto. This time, I found a Mexican girlfriend who showed me the town and the campo, introduced me to her friends, and life here became vibrant for me. I met a lovely black woman of Haitian descent. She became my first adult black friend and loved joking with me about my Southern heritage, calling me Billy Wayne Redneck. She was both brilliant and terribly sad. Unforgettable.

My third summer in 1960 was even better. By then I was growing as a writer. Like so many of the people in this book, I was captivated by the people and the place and the complex culture.

Through the years after college, after working for a Nashville singer/songwriter and a New York publisher, I returned to the South. In 1967, while working as a reporter, my first novel was published. After a stint at Harvard as a Nieman Fellow with my new wife, a young lawyer, we went home to Alabama. A year or so later we traveled to Mexico where I eagerly introduced her to "the place where the sky turns blue." We stayed in the Posada Ermita, met the owner, the Mexican movie star Cantinflas, and hiked through the cobblestone streets like we owned them. Sally not only enjoyed the town, she felt at home in La Cucaracha, where Chucho hugged her with a warm San Miguel welcome.

Late in the 70s, after the publication of my third book, I became a free-lance writer. During the 1980s and 90s, I wrote numerous travel articles for *The New York Times* and other newspapers and magazines, returning to Mexico and San Miguel many times to see my old friends, particularly Stirling Dickinson. At dinner I would hear what he'd been doing. He was always interesting and always interested.

After my wife Sally retired as circuit judge in 2003, we rented a house here. Later that year we bought a house in the Ojo de Agua neighborhood. Since then we have divided our time between here and Montgomery. Each year, it seems, we spend more time in San Miguel and enjoy it more and more. Each year, our little Havanese, Ellie, who has been making the trip with us since she was a small puppy, enjoys it as much. Each of John Scherber's interviews sings to me. Each is a gem. Each shines with its own inner brightness.

As I read his manuscript, I was touched by every individual, some I have known, all of whom I now know because this marvelous interviewer has allowed their voices to be heard. His book is a fabulous surprise that glows, like its subjects, and it has entered a special place in my heart.

Wayne Greenhaw
San Miguel de Allende

INTRODUCTION

Any map will show that Mexico inhabits the lower extremity of the North American continent, along with its neighbors of Central America. It will suggest that it resembles an upright cornucopia supporting the land masses of the United States and Canada, ending in the tail of a mermaid thrust upward into the Caribbean Sea. While accurate, these things are not much use in finding its true location, because for many who live here, Mexico is a place in the heart.

Viewed from a distance, it is the shape of your best hope. From a closer perspective it lies somewhere in the right atrium or the left ventricle—it varies for different people. It is often on the first left after the Source of Dreams, whose precise location has never been determined, but whose function can be powerful. It is either a new beginning or a dead end. It can be a place to be poor as easily as a place to be rich. It can be a place to die as well as a place to live. It can be any or all of these things for anyone, and it can differ from day to day. It often does.

This is a book made up of stories Americans and Canadians have told me about why they settled in Mexico, and what it means to them. These may not be like the stories they heard from others before they came, or the fantasies that brought them here originally. Usually they aren't. Many Americans are here as tourists, some are here as renters part of the year, others own homes here but maintain a base in the States as well. I have confined this book to the stories of expatriates who live here full time, as I do. They may have family in the States or Canada, they probably keep their assets there, but they live in Mexico year round and maintain no real estate footprint north of the border. This necessarily involves a different relationship with a foreign country.

This book was driven by questions I began to ask myself after I'd lived in Mexico for eight months. What was my relationship with the political life of the States as I watched a new presidential campaign unfold? How long would it be before I felt like going back for a visit? What had I given up to come here, and what had I gained? What was my new role in this community? Was I an exile? An expatriate? Would I ever live in the States again? How did I react to Americans I saw here visiting?

What had I done?

In sum, what are the real costs and benefits of doing something like this? On the day I arrived I could have asked myself none of these questions. Now I can ask them, but answering many of them has eluded me. This is what drove me to ask others.

My purpose in doing this book was not to conduct a survey, nor was it a way of ranking the features of Mexico on a scale of one to ten, or comparing it with any other place. My sample is much too small to aim at being scientific. Instead it hopes to illustrate at an individual level for a number of different people what it really means to make a change like this, the feelings and emotions it evokes, the economic and social realities that come with it, the challenges to old identities or the blossoming of new ones that are inevitable in a different culture. It is personal and anecdotal.

Mexico is a country of tremendous diversity, and the mix of colonial heritage, regional differences, and the base of 8,000 or more Americans living in San Miguel de Allende make that city unique. While many things the reader finds in this book will apply to all of Mexico, bear in mind that some will not. If I had interviewed expatriates in Oaxaca or Ajijic on Lake Chapala, it would have been a different book. When you consider a place to live, there is no substitute for your own careful research.

On the plane trip down here I sat next to a man and his wife returning from Houston. He was in his eighties and frail. She told me they had returned for a medical procedure connected with a fall he had taken on the steps of their home here. Afterward they had sold their two-story house in San Miguel de Allende and bought a single story house. A month later I saw him on the street, navigating the cobblestones with difficulty, but he was still here, although it clearly would have been easier to leave.

Others have suggested there is a six or seven year time frame when people hit the wall. Some leave after a few months thinking they never should have come. Those thinking of buying a home here are well advised to rent for a while first.

As I had these conversations I realized there was a different San Miguel for each person I talked to. It went beyond the merely subjective. It was about identity, race, culture, politics, art. It was about sufficiency and abundance, and it was about the meaning of family and the path to fulfillment.

It was about exploring a place in the heart.

CHAPTER 1

I HAD A DREAM

I s there any reason to pay attention to a dream? Not the kind Martin Luther King spoke of, where the word really meant *hope*. I mean a nasty, gritty, in your face kind of dream that threatens to upend every part of your life. A dream with a lethal message spoken by a strangely dressed messenger who walks up to you without warning while, of all things, you are window shopping with a friend.

"The reason I came here is because I had a dream," says Linda Vandiver, as we sit in the studio she shares with her son Kelley, who, like Linda, is a painter.

"We all have a dream," I respond, not unkindly, thinking of a heartrending, soul-bearing interview that might be just over the next hill. That's my dream.

"I mean a *real* dream," she says bluntly. "I was supervisor of histology and cytology in a huge hospital in Tulsa, Oklahoma. I had a tremendous amount of responsibility, and I had a dream that I was walking down the street speaking with my best friend, and I was complaining about all the stuff that I was having to do at the hospital, where we had just moved the histology department. That involved working twenty-four hours a day and

1

keeping the department running as we moved it.

"I had a federal inspection coming up in a month, and I was complaining that, oh my gosh, this is hard, and she said to me, in the dream, what would you have to do to move to San Miguel? And I answered as we were kind of window shopping while we moved down the street, 'I'd have to give up my retirement since I'm not vested at this hospital—it takes ten years—I wouldn't have health care anymore, and I'd have to sell my house and my car.' Right about then this man came walking toward me right in front of me. He was dressed as a Hassidic Jewish rabbi, which you don't see in Tulsa, Oklahoma.

"I was looking at him and I moved to let him by and he moved over in front of me. He put his hand on my arm and it was icy cold and he said, 'Are you Linda Vandiver?' I said 'yes,' and he said, 'I have a message for you.' I said, 'Is it that I should go to San Miguel?'"

"He said, 'That's not my message. My message is you have only seven months left to live.'"

It is the highly specific nature of the message that freezes me in my chair. It's not a voice borne on the wind, it's a rabbi with a beard and long black coat and hat standing on a Tulsa sidewalk. The prediction is not, you've got maybe a year or so, maybe more. It's a flat seven months. Why seven? It's as if the man truly *knows.*

Linda was fifty-two on that night, and she is not Jewish. She was raised Catholic and has never been an Old Testament scholar. In college she had a double major in art and biology, thinking to be a medical illustrator.

"I woke up scared to death. I went to work and I kept thinking all day, seven months is a strange amount of time. I came home from work and I meditated, maybe ten, fifteen minutes, and I had the realization that if this were true, and I only had seven months to live, would I live like I was living? I knew the answer would be no."

Her voice trails off here and she is looking, not at me, but over my shoulder, back at one of those rarely identifiable true turning points, a pinpoint in time, where you can say, "After that day everything was different."

"I realized that it wouldn't matter if I had health care, it wouldn't matter if I sold my house and my car, that what would matter would be doing what made me happy, and not working so hard. If I really only had seven months to live, then I'm going to live my life as if I had only seven months to live. I took about a month and painted and fixed up my house and got it ready. I had been divorced in the 1980s. I had bought this little house in Oklahoma, and I'd be owing money on it until I was seventy-six years old. It just hit me that day that I'd have to *work* until I was seventy-six years old.

"I wouldn't want to do that, I'd want to be free. I'd want to live my life differently. It was a big, important dream in my life. I put my house on the market and at the first open house it sold. The people were from San Luis Potosi, Mexico."

The funds for the transaction had to come from Mexico, and they were going to take a while to process. At this time Linda was working for eight pathologists, and she said nothing to them for two months. When everything was approved she gave four months notice.

"They all said I was crazy. It *was* a frightening thing to do."

But did her family support the idea?

"Everyone was pretty shocked. My father had

3

Alzheimer's Disease. My mother felt like I was deserting her. My kids were upset with me."

Linda is the only girl among three siblings. It would be her traditional role to stay close to home and help out, and she might have done that if she hadn't been under a death sentence.

"I explained to my mother that my husband had been military and I'd moved all over the world all the time and I'd never really done with my life what I wanted to do. It seemed imperative at that age that I could. I knew since I'd sold my house I could give my youngest son [money] for his last year in college. Then I could come down here and begin all over. "It was a pretty scary thing to do because I only got $250 a month from my ex-husband's military retirement."

Just before she left her job she decided to have a physical exam while she was still covered by insurance. Doctors discovered a tumor in her breast. It was December of 1993. Six months after the dream, it suddenly looked like the rabbi had been right.

"At first I was terrified because it looked like it was going to be true. Then I realized, you know, I'm really lucky. I've sold everything, I've given away everything I treasured. If it's malignant, I can travel and do whatever I want. This was meant to be. So I was totally at peace with it. I just decided that whatever it was, it was going to be all right.

"It was a pre-malignant tumor, not malignant yet, but I'm sure it would have been."

The tumor was removed, so small she wouldn't have found it herself.

Linda had known about San Miguel since the 80s,

when she had come down with a doctor she worked with who had been given the use of a house here for a week. Linda found that she loved it. It was an artist's colony and it reconnected her with her old dreams of painting.

"I made the joke that when my kids were out of college I was just going to be a hippie artist. Later I came in the early 90s with my son Kelley to visit, and that reinforced the fact that I thought this was what I wanted to do. Then my uncle retired from the Medical College of Virginia and he came here to live. That was another inspiration, that I would have a little bit of family here."

The uncle knew about San Miguel because Linda had told him after her first visit. When she arrived his place served as a base. "When I first came I stayed with my uncle until I found an apartment that I could afford. It was hard because I had for so many years lived on a schedule, be at work at five A.M., go to breakfast at 8:30, go to lunch at 12:00. You have fifteen minutes for the coffee break. I've lived my life like this. When I first got here I made myself work [at painting], like from eight in the morning until noon. Then I'd make myself work until five. I disciplined myself, I just really lived by my old rules. The hardest thing for me was that I didn't have any friends, I'd left all my family."

In January her youngest son slipped on a patch of ice and tore ligaments in his knee. She didn't have the money to go back and be there for him, and he ended up staying with his roommate's family. It was the same month she arrived. "I felt that everything happens the way it's supposed to, I just have to deal with this, he has to learn to grow up and I have to learn to let go."

Now, fifteen years later, she is something of a

hermit, not connected much with cultural or volunteer groups. While she has friends in both the American and Mexican communities, the casual contacts she enjoys most are the conversations with visitors who come into the gallery.

She lives in a Mexican neighborhood called Obraje, where for many years there was only one other American. She bought a lot soon after her arrival with money she had left from selling her house, thinking it might be an investment. Five years later, she returned to the States to work for ten months back at the hospital in Tulsa, living at her mother's house. The woman who had replaced her had contracted cancer and they were desperate. With the money she saved during that period she was able to build a house on her property when she returned. A small house doesn't cost much in Mexico, and she'd been paid well to return.

"I think the first month I was there was probably the most horrible of my life. It had been five years, and I couldn't remember the computer codes. I had just totally shut the door on it all. When I left there had been 22,000 cases and seven techs, and when I came back I had four registered techs and two that were learning, and we did 38,000 cases. It was hard, but I did it because I wanted to earn the money to build a little house."

I raise the issue of whether that experience might have revealed more to her about the States after being gone for five years, or about her life in San Miguel.

"It was both. What I realized...was that I had gotten myself in a place [before] where I owed on my house and on my car and...you just spend all of your money on *things* and you don't realize it. It's a way of life. And it's a choice.

"Down here I got up when I wanted, I went to bed when I wanted. I joined the Unity Church when I got down here to meet people. I think I was here three months when I met a woman at Unity Church who was beside me who was teary, and I hugged her. The next day, on my lunch hour that I allowed myself, I was just outside my door when I ran into this woman. She hugged me and she said how important it was that I had hugged her and did I have time to talk to her. I felt myself really torn, [thinking] oh, I only have an hour, I just can't, and then I knew I should.

"I invited her in and she was in my house three hours. I ran my errands after she left; I rigged up some lights, and I was able to continue working my time for that day. When I went to bed I had this realization that everything had unfolded the way it was supposed to. What was I doing? When I got up the next morning she had written a poem to me that was slid under my door. I realized that life was too short to do what I was doing, that I was continuing my hectic United States pace, and I didn't need to do it."

It was at this point that the measured pace of Mexico took over her life. She had already stopped paying much attention to U.S. news. She didn't own a TV set and found herself being more peaceful and happy being out of the loop. It was as if it was all on a need to know basis, and she didn't need to. In this year of presidential politics she has, at least, followed the primaries. Now, after 15 years in San Miguel, she watches news on her computer. "I get disgusted still, I don't understand the United States, but that's about it. I hope there can be a change. But I'm *here*."

I ask Linda to amplify the part about not understanding the U.S.

"What I don't understand is the fear people had from 9/11 on, including one of my sons, who was a marine. To me it's just against who I am. I don't want to have fear, and I don't want to live in fear. That, plus the materialism. You know, when I was at the hospital and watching my friends, I said, 'you all have got to pay off your bills so that you're free. You can't leave, because you owe.'

"I can live on my social security here, and I took it at sixty-two I don't have health insurance; it doesn't bother me in the slightest. I'm just happy."

It seems pointless to ask, but does Linda know of anything that would make her go back to the U.S.? Possibly some change in Mexico that would make her feel unwelcome or insecure? All I get in response is a vague shrug. Mexico is home.

"I feel safe in my neighborhood. You can tell, there's a family or two, the young ones, they don't like Americans. But the parents are not that way."

Where would she be, if she weren't in Mexico?

"I might be in Tibet, volunteering. I might be in Peru, doing the same." She laughs.

By being here she feels she has only given up the closeness of her family, and seeing her grand kids more often. Nothing else.

Linda's studio is in the *Fabrica la Aurora*, a former textile mill that sprawls informally over a number of acres on the north side of town. Her back wall is a traditional Mexican stone design using large flat irregular stones set in mortar with small stones embedded around them. Walls like this are attractive but not water tight. Now moisture seeps through from the recent heavy rains, and a ceiling fan runs as we talk.

Her paintings are large vivid floral subjects realistically rendered. The big mullioned window in front faces a sunny concrete plaza within the old factory. Other studios are visible, a covered coffee and sandwich shop run by three attractive young Mexican women, and the back entrance of an upscale furniture and accessories store. Other shops offer Mexican antiques and religious art. In the center is a small bookstore, focused on design. There is a village feeling to the complex. Outside is a large parking lot, something almost unknown in this town other than at the few big box stores at the outskirts. At the end of the parking lot is a fenced area full of ducks of several varieties with their own pool. It doesn't provoke much comment although the reason it's there isn't obvious.

While she feels this environment is a good fit, Linda also knows she is different from many Americans who live In San Miguel. "I don't have very much money. I have a little adobe home. I live in a Mexican neighborhood, I live on my retirement, on social security. Many of them, when I first came and I was invited to parties, recognized I didn't fit. I'm not a drinker, I'm not a partygoer. If I go to a party I want to meet people I have something in common with. I want to talk to them about things that are important to me, not food, not houses."

Her social set tends to be other artists and what she calls, "spiritual seekers."

"I was in a women's group for years, and they are basically very spiritual women. Some are Mexican, others are different nationalities."

She has some Mexican friends, although her best

Mexican friend died this year. She agrees, however, as others have said, that none of these friends are in the first tier of her relationships. I ask if she knows why.

"I guess there's an issue with us, that they don't trust us." She agrees that it might be the many years of bad history between the two countries.

"My Mexican friend who just died had an American father, so she spoke English and Spanish. She lived here all her life. I didn't have that problem with her, she was my best friend. My other Mexican friends, they would do anything for me. I don't feel a separation from them as far as that they judge me. I don't know what it is, unless it's that we don't have a tremendous amount in common. I don't know.

"I don't have much of a social life. I have dated. I used to go to all the Mexican functions downtown and now it's like it's not high on my list. When I first came a friend of mine invited me to La Fragua [a restaurant bar, near the *jardin*, our central plaza]. I went, dragging my feet the whole way, and actually I loved it. Americans went on Friday night; there were a lot of Americans there, a lot of Mexicans. It used to be the *Romanticos* [a trio playing traditional Mexican songs] were there. I just loved them, they're my friends. I love to dance and I used to go there and dance every Friday, Saturday and Sunday night. Saturday night was Mexican night, almost all Mexicans. "Sunday night I would go with an American friend of mine who was a really good dancer who's been here longer than I have. That used to be my social life, and it was really fun."

I ask how, as a long time resident, she relates to the American tourists she encounters.

"I have a lot of tourists come in here. There are different kinds. Some are wonderful people that I love to connect with. Usually they're people who want to know why am I here? How is it different? What makes me happy here? It's a real pleasure to talk to those people because they're also waking up and realizing, what am I doing with my life? I'm spending everything I make on more things.

"Part of having a gallery for me, in fact, the reason I still do this, is because I meet a lot of wonderful people, and I feel that I'm able to touch people many times. It might only be one person a month, but it's somebody that will sit down here and say, why are you here? What makes you happy here? Then you know you've actually spoken your heart to someone. Mexico, for me—I can get off the plane coming from the States having had a wonderful time—two weeks, three weeks is max, and I want to be home. As soon as I hit San Miguel, it's like [she exhales enormously, as if a weight has been lifted, her neck and shoulder muscles suddenly loosening] I just relax, and I recognize it; it's almost an instantaneous feeling. Wow, I'm home! It just feels that way here to me."

What kind of journey is this? From the high intensity pace of running a histology and cytology lab for a major hospital to running a small studio/gallery in a middling Mexican hill town. What changes have come about in Linda Vandiver herself along the way?

"I live for my heart now. I am able to ask myself, how do I feel about this? What should I really do? What's important to me? What matters? Before, I was in a rat race. I didn't have time to ask myself those questions. I didn't have time to say, if I had only six months left to live what would I do with it? It never occurred to me. I was busy; I didn't have time to smell the roses."

She thinks back to her first year here. A problem for many of us is to understand what we are seeing, since so much of it is unfamiliar. Everything is foreign in this place that is right on our border, but a world away in its thinking.

"I was still living with my uncle and the neighbors invited me for a special dinner. He was a mechanic and she sold little things when school got out [a vendor of snacks at the edge of the school grounds]. She had three children, and we were all around the table having dinner. It was a very special dinner she had cooked, and I felt so honored because I knew they were poor. While we were eating dinner someone knocked at the door.

"She answered the door and an old lady came in and was asking if they had any extra food. My neighbor pulled another chair and brought the lady to the table and sat her down. She got her a Coke and brought her a plate of food. And I went home and I cried. I still cry because it touched me so much. That's when I realized that this is where I ought to be. I knew I would stay here.

"You know, after I quit my job I had two different, really significant job offers, that any time before I quit I would have really wanted to have. It was almost as if the universe was testing me to me to see if I really was going to follow my heart."

❊❊❊

I believe that Linda Vandiver was so deeply *embedded* in her Tulsa life that she was unable to consciously ask the questions that came up in her dream. The demanding job, where finding a replacement for her skills was nearly impossible, the role of single parent of four children, where she had been their principal emotional and financial support, had long made the concept of change inconceivable. It was only after the rabbi condemned her to death that her constraints receded and she was able to confront the issue on a conscious level.

Linda's question from her meditation on the day after her fateful dream stays with me. "If I had only seven months to live, would I live like I was living?" Take out the words, "seven months," and insert the words, "the rest of my life."

It could apply to any of us.

CHAPTER 2

WE'RE NOT IN THE BUBBLE ANYMORE

There's a small tunnel just off the Querétaro road, one car wide with a brick barrel vault ceiling. The incline appears to be about forty-five degrees. It's easy to miss, and even if you didn't miss it, it doesn't look like something you'd want to attempt without sherpas. I tried it once, after a party, and was even able to turn around and come back down front-end first. It took considerable prompting. Returning for this conversation, however, I knew what to expect so I took a cab.

At the top of this slope, Mike and Louise live on the edge of the basin that holds San Miguel in its cupped hands. Their house is terraced down over three levels and scans a view that sweeps the entire city and the two or three levels of mountains beyond. It's a view you could rent by the minute, and it stops just short of forever. This is why they call the house *Casa Mirador.*

In a covered *ramada* at the end of a wide curving terrace we settle in to talk about why they would ever pick a place like this to come to earth when they could have stayed in Texas with the air conditioning on.

Louise tackles the question. "Mike is a retired doctor [Radiology and Nuclear Medicine]. He retired early. We lived in Dallas. He looked at Costa Rica, Portugal and Spain."

"And Panama," he adds. Living in Mexico has not caused his command of detail to dry up. "We came down here for a vacation. Three days later, he bought a house, a little house on Reloj and we started coming back and forth, and [once when we came back] to Dallas, he said "I want to move down there." I said, "If you want to move I'll move with you, but we need a big house because we have all these kids."

"I've known about San Miguel for better than fifteen years, says Mike "from all the travel magazines recommending various retirement spots around the world. The attraction was geographic. It was relatively close, a nonstop flight from either Dallas or Houston. The quality of life was great; the weather is superior to anything in Texas. The final decision was mainly economic."

Mike had studied Spanish for two years both in high school and college. Louise had some informal Spanish at that point.

"I'm Italian," she says. "I spent a lot of time in Mexico. I was in the airline industry, so I can make myself understood, and we find that if you try, they really appreciate it. One of these days I'll go to school."

They ended up renovating the house on Reloj and then leasing it out about half time, which covered all the operating expenses. Mike recalls making the transition from vacation home to permanent residence. "When we decided to come down full time in January of 2005 we spent a very frustrating week looking at property, scores of properties, and the evening before we were scheduled to leave, one of the real estate agents called and said, 'You know, there's a spec house on the mountain you might want to go look at."

"It was about 30% built," Louise adds.

"I came up with the real estate agent and said, 'Wow, these views are pretty stunning.' The house was very vertical, it's a long walk up, but we're still young enough and walking is not that much of a chore for us. Louise took a taxi up and she said yes, size-wise it looks good. So we thought about it a while."

"We were very lucky," Louise says, "because we were able to put in the house what we wanted to. The builder was very good to us."

"Very flexible," says Mike.

"We picked everything that we wanted to make our life comfortable here, so it worked out really well. We're very happy here. Who could not love this view? They call us the twenty-tens. It's twenty pesos up by taxi and a ten minute walk down."

The only obstacle to moving down to San Miguel for Louise was leaving her kids and seven grandchildren. The kids themselves were supportive of the move, but she knew she would miss watching the grand kids grow up. "The thing that really let me say OK and let go of Dallas was that it was only an hour and a half by plane. I was just back in Dallas for three weeks, and I said to my son, 'You know, I have made better friends in San Miguel than I ever had in Dallas.'

"I really shouldn't say that because I have wonderful friends in Dallas, but what happens I think as you get older is that you change a little bit. The women down here especially are incredibly adventurous. And they're flexible; we have so much in common."

For Mike, settling in full time fully lived up to all his expectations. "There's so much going on, you could be busy seven days a week, not only in the afternoon, but the evenings as well. This place is magical, and everyone is wonderful. We've had—not we personally—but the city has had a few crime issues. That's never touched us."

Louise leans back in her chair and looks out over the city. "What this is, is a place that is very easy to live in. The weather is gorgeous. The people are wonderful. We seem to be welcomed by the Mexican people. I think we're adding to the economy. I think especially from a charitable standpoint the Americans are helping San Miguel an awful lot."

I wonder about getting close to Mexicans socially, as friends and equals.

"If you put yourself out and you want to, sure. We have several friends that…"

"Well," Louise jumps in, "we don't have that many. I think that they want to stay by themselves. We have a few Mexican friends. Our architect is a good friend of ours. I think that they like what we do for the community."

"If I wanted to put myself out to make friends with a Mexican family," says Mike, "or several Mexican men, I could do that, and I'm sure that they'd reciprocate. I don't think it's as absolute as Louise's statement implies. There is some of it, no question, and many of them, even the upper middle class folks, are a little bit standoffish, but if you put yourself out and you have common interests…"

"There was a young lady," adds Louise, "who painted our ceiling in here. She's an artist; her name is Socorro. She looks like she's twenty and she's, like, thirty-eight. She has seven children. She's a very Catholic woman, but when I saw her on her back painting the ceiling it was just amazing.

"She said to me one day, 'would you come to my house please?' She lives out there in La Luz. She said, 'I'd really like you to meet my children.' So I walked in and there were these seven children. The house was spotless; they were wonderful. Her husband is a musician, her son plays the piano, three children sing, her other son plays the violin. And they all performed for me. What an experience that was!

"But as far as inviting them for dinner or them inviting us for dinner, I don't think that would happen. Do you?" she asks Mike.

"Actually," says Mike, "Socorro and her husband and one of the children came for lunch one day."

"Was that Socorro or was that Oswaldo?"

The point I take from this is that these get-togethers can happen and probably more than once, because they are not so remarkable that everyone remembers exactly who came when.

Mike is committed to supporting most of the volunteer agencies in town financially through his charitable trust.

"I was involved with one of the orphanages here when I first came down," Louisa says. "I raised a lot of money for them, and hit up my friends in the States. There was a woman here, Sally, who devoted like five years of her life to this orphanage. I became friends with her and started doing some fund raising and raised quite a bit of money. We said we would like you to devote this money to building a computer room. It was what the kids wanted. And we were going to build a new kitchen. We got the builder here to donate a lot of money.

"Well, it happened that they had a change in the nuns, and a new nun came in and wouldn't allow Sally to do anything." Louise shrugs in a way that is not quite Mexican.

"Even if I contribute as often as every six months," says Mike, "it seems as if the entire board has changed. Every six months it seems to roll over. People say, 'Well, I'm going to do this,' but obviously they either get burned out or are unhappy with the performance, and there is a lot of staff change."

"We did get involved," says Louise, "with Casita Linda, [a group that builds houses for homeless families], and that's a wonderful organization. Mike has built a couple of houses for them."

I wonder how Mike feels about all the turnover in these organizations.

"Well, I have no control over it, obviously. My role is basically limited to a financial one. I think financially they're all fairly capable; I don't think there's any kind of fraud. It's a big responsibility. You've not only got to collect the money, you've got put it into practice. The places we contribute—Casita Linda's easy because all they do is build houses. The others, the SPA and Amigos Animales, they spay and neuter, so that's pretty straight forward. The Hospice, obviously they do what they do, and that's demanding."

"I think," adds Louise, "a lot of the larger charities are a little political, I do."

"Feed the Hungry and Patronato por Niños provide medical and dental care for children. Again, I really have no interest in jumping in and driving meals out to the *campo*. I'm not interested in that. I'd much rather give financial support and let them deal with it. I have no personal need to be involved, I guess is what I'm saying."

These efforts do not represent their entire involvement with the problem of poverty in San Miguel. "We have two full time employees as well," says Mike.

"We do a lot for the employees too, above and beyond what you're supposed to do, and what the government says you have to do. They're wonderful and we love them. They seem to enjoy working for us." She laughs.

In terms of how they find themselves now relative to the U.S., Mike sees the question partly in terms of assets. "I have all of my assets in the U.S. now, our financial assets. I have no real estate, and if the U.S. economy takes a change in January, after the election, I'm prepared to move what assets I still have in the U.S. overseas."

"I still have a house there," says Louise.

"In March," adds Mike, "I'll be eligible for the citizenship test, which I plan to take. I'll have dual citizenship. I'll still vote in the U.S.; an expat can vote at his or her last permanent address."

Both Mike and Louise strongly reject the idea that they are staying in touch less since they moved to Mexico. Mike reads *The New York Times* every day and *The Wall Street Journal*. Even if they moved the financial assets out of the States that would not affect their need to stay informed.

"My primary modus operandi is financial," he says. "That's the reason I'm here. My house in Dallas that I lived in for twenty-five years was built in 1959, and it was getting a little bit long in the tooth. I put a new roof on four or five years before I left and put a new top-end heating and air conditioning unit in, which saved a lot of money. Those kinds of expenses I was looking at every two or three years. Plus, with no income tax in the state of Texas, property taxes are fairly substantial. Louise and I jointly were paying $19,000 a year. The property taxes here are $400 a year."

I pause and look back over the house and gardens. They could be material for a spread in any residential design magazine.

"A lot of my dealings were financial, and that was part of the reason why I decided to retire. My medical liability insurance, never having been sued, never even having been named in a suit, in 2001 was $8800, in 2002 was $19,000, and in 2003 was $38,000. I also worked as an expert witness for a very prominent law firm in Dallas. Three or four times a years they'd send me something to look at, and half or two-thirds of the time it might go to deposition. I never went to trial because it was pretty black and white, never very gray."

Mike returns to see family two or three times a year, Louise more often, either to see her grandchildren or for a medical reason. His views on the local medical services are that they run the gamut, just as in the U.S. "Mexico City is certainly first world medicine. Angeles (Hospital in Querétaro) is mixed, but there's some good stuff going on there. There's not so good stuff going there as well."

Louise is completely unable to think of anything that would make her move back to the States, other than something happening to one of her children. "Or if I got to the point where I needed medical care, not caretakers, because I think you could get better care down here. The custodial care here would be wonderful because the Mexicans are so compassionate and caring. Custodial, I think, down here would be perfect."

"Nothing would draw me back at this point," adds Mike.

Louise still works at her executive search business, something she can handle easily at this distance with a computer and Vonnage. With her son, she has also built a spec home in San Miguel.

As for what this city offers that Dallas didn't, weather is the first thing to come up. "It was 106 degrees when I was in Dallas last week," says Louise. The statement stands with no further embellishment.

Mike makes a sweeping gesture over the slope that includes most of San Miguel. "The cost of living, the quality of life. I don't even wear a watch; I tell time by the calendar."

"We entertain a lot," she adds. "We have a lot of friends who come to visit us. It's as social as you want it to be. You can do as much as you want; you can hole up and read a book if you don't want to do anything. Our kids can come, we can travel. But for the people who are living on social security, I don't know if it would be right. Ajijic, perhaps. For myself there's no way I could have lived there [in Dallas] the way I live here, even though I was doing very well, but it's not all about finances."

"In my mind," adds Mike, "a lot of the decision came down to finances, because at age fifty-eight, when I retired, I had no property tax relief for another seven years. At age sixty-five they would have frozen my independent school district tax at that level. In Texas the school taxes are two-thirds or three-quarters of the total."

Now, the only thing Louise misses are her children. She is able to work as much as she wants doing her searches. There's nothing else that she misses. "We do travel quite a bit. I'm not sure if we were still in Dallas that we'd do the traveling that we do. We spent two weeks in Turkey and six weeks in Africa this year. We're going to New York and New England next month. Then, of course, the beach in December. I'm giving up nothing."

"We have parties," adds Louise, "like for fifty people. We can set up tables out here and it doesn't cost a whole lot of money. You can't do that in the States."

Some people have said to me that San Miguel is a stratified society. I wonder if they have identified their strata.

"The gangs of San Miguel?" Louise asks immediately. "We do a little bit of everything."

"We chose," says Mike, "we knew there were organized cliques, and they virtually never interacted, so we chose to remain apart from each of those entities. I haven't been in Harry's [possibly the headquarters of the cocktail clique] in four years. We interact with everybody and one week we'll support this, and the next week we'll do that."

Louise nods in agreement. "When we first came down here a friend said, 'You know, there are cliques down here. The cliques just don't mix.' She's been here fifteen years. She said it's better if you just don't get involved with the cliques. When we have a party here we invite people from everywhere. That's the best way to be, I think. We certainly don't want to get into a class distinction or anything like that."

"We've lived through that," says Mike. "When you're younger and you're raising your children, just by virtue of the fact that you have children you're sort of boxed into a social group that also has children. Especially when they're in a private school, then you've got to get involved with fund raising."

"It's a bubble," adds Louise. "We lived in Highland Park [a Dallas suburb], that's where I raised my kids, and I don't ever want to live in a bubble again."

Mike and Louise are quite welcoming to tourists; Mike spends time on the Internet communicating with people about to come down, offering recommendations and other information.

"We've met some wonderful people, and several of them, in fact, have bought houses here and live here part time. Some people are just coming for their first trip and they say can you help me? If I help them they say, Do you want to go out for a glass of wine or a cup of coffee?"

Louise has a story about their neighbors in a rental house next door. She was having a dinner party and one of her guests had not appeared. She wanted to call but her phone wasn't working, so she went next door. "I go over and knock on their door and say, 'Can I use your phone? I am so angry!' I didn't know these people, but I said, 'You know, I've got all this food, come on over and eat.'

"They said they'd love to. He was Richard Lourie, and he's written an awful lot of books. One of them was just on *The New York Times* list. The last one he wrote was *A Hatred for Tulips*."

"It was a fictional account of the betrayal of Anne Frank," adds Mike. "They both have Ph.D.s from

Berkeley; his is in Russian."

"We really hit it off," says Louise. "He writes for a Russian newspaper. We got to be good friends with them and they invited us out to New York, and that's how these things happen. They bought a house here within three days."

"We referred them to a real estate agent; they saw twenty houses and bought one."

"Now they live here six months a year. But the other interesting story is from doing searches for the airline industry. About ten years ago I placed this guy as a vice president of Air France, and we stayed in touch. One day he called me—this must have been about three or four years ago. He said, 'I'm getting burned out. Find me a job.' I said, 'There's a restaurant for sale here, why don't you come to San Miguel?' So he and Patrice came down, stayed with us for about three weeks, and bought Romano's."

So how have Mike and Louise changed since they've lived here?

"I've become much more relaxed," she answers.

"Our outlook, our perspective on life is a lot broader than it was," Mike adds. "Of course we travel now so much. When you're working for a living you don't get an opportunity to travel unless you're traveling on business. Now it's different. We can spontaneously pick up and go, and we have. We've been virtually everywhere in the world except Australia and New Zealand in the last four years."

"But I think personally we've both relaxed a whole lot. Nothing bothers me any more."

I ask her whether it's partly about the inability to

control life here as much as it was possible back in Texas.

"I really think that Mike has lost a lot of that. Being what he was, his profession, he had to be controlling. That was one of things that bothered me more than anything was his wanting to control everything. But you've let go of that a lot. It's like, why worry about it, you know? You reach a certain age and I'm just not going to worry. I'll worry about my health, I'll worry about my children, but that's about it."

"The Mexican lifestyle forces you to relax," says Mike. "You can't take anything terribly seriously. If somebody says, and you've got a problem with your house, I'll be there to look at it on Friday, well, there's a lot of Fridays. I've learned to accept that and I don't even care anymore." Mike begins to shake with laughter as he stares off at the meandering profile of the mountains near Guanajuato.

"Well, the first couple years we cared," says Louise. "The first couple years we were saying, why can't they fix this, why can't they do it right now! But you learn to say, they'll fix it eventually.

"But I think the friendships we've developed down here have added so much to our lives. They are friendships you develop with people from other parts of the country, other parts of the world. They add so much to your life. You're not in that bubble anymore. You're dealing with all kinds of people from all walks of life, and they all have stories. Some of them reinvent themselves, like the woman who was married to the army sergeant and..."

"...ended up in San Miguel," Mike finishes, "as the widow of a navy admiral."

"And that's OK," says Louise, "whatever floats your boat."

For Mike and Louise the experience of meeting the Richard Louries typifies the San Miguel experience. "You leave yourself wide open," he says, "and you can meet these incredible people and develop just a wonderful friendship with them. It's just different. I don't think we could ever do that before, where would we meet the people we've met because in the States you're in your own bubble, and you never get out of it. Here you can go anywhere, you can talk to anybody."

"Sure, if we were still in Dallas," adds Mike, "we'd have lots of attorney friends, we'd have lots of physician friends, but we didn't know anybody in the artistic community in Dallas. I knew the names of famous people, but I didn't know them personally at all."

"You gain so much from other people. But is San Miguel going to get too big, too cosmopolitan?"

It seems that it plays both ways. The growth, the cosmopolitan atmosphere that makes it easy to meet interesting people also threatens the little shopkeepers whose numbers decrease monthly as the big box stores come in. Even in the five years Mike and Louise have been here the changes are clear, and not always welcome. A few big things are gained and many small things are lost.

They keep an eye on the changes from their perch on the edge of the hillside, where they can also see nearly to Guatemala.

CHAPTER 3

FOR A FEW DOLLARS MORE

It took Bob Fredericks nearly twenty-eight years to get from Sarasota to San Miguel, but it wasn't the traffic.

"I heard about it the first time in the fall of 1975. I was practicing dentistry, and I had a patient who had a house here. They would come here in the summer because it was too hot in Florida, and too humid. She told me all about the place. I wrote the name down and created a manila folder. Every time there was an article about San Miguel I'd put it in that folder. Of course, I was thirty or forty years away from retirement."

I ask whether it was the climate.

"It was the culture. To me it sounded like Sarasota--a little town with an opera company, an art school, a liberal arts college--there were extraordinary things to do there." The file was fairly thick by the time Bob visited for the first time in 2003.

"As I got older and social security was a possibility, I started doing the numbers and thought, how am I going to live in the Bay Area on social security? [By this time he had relocated to Oakland, CA.] I had a condo. The condo fees and taxes were $200 a month, and with the mortgage payment it totaled my income [once he retired] on social security. I thought, I don't want to work until the day I die; living in the Bay Area is not an option. So I started looking—I always want something exotic.

"I took a trip to Costa Rica, and I found that the only place that had culture was San Jose, the capital, a yucky place. The really attractive places are on either coast, and by that time it was already expensive to buy land and build. I thought about Belize, but I never went there after I read a couple of articles about piracy and crime."

While Bob was agonizing about his choices, with a growing awareness that it was time to decide something, two neighbors in his condo building were preparing for a week-long trip to San Miguel. Each was planning to buy a house. When they invited him to come along, he dusted off the manila folder.

"We were here seven days. They each bought a house, and I bought a lot." He doesn't sound surprised. This was in 2003. He hadn't looked at other towns in Mexico, although he'd heard about Lake Chapala, and it didn't seem right. "What appealed to me here was that they had art schools, music festivals. It was a small town that had all of the big city advantages, and it looked like it was really affordable."

He was already taking Spanish in night school.

With the assistance of a Mexican woman who ran a beauty shop and also sold real estate, he was able to view a large number of properties that didn't appear in the windows of the high end realtors downtown. "That's how I found these lots. Both of the houses that my friends bought were in Independencia. One was $50,000, the other was $60,000. My lot was purchased from a young

29

Mexican man, and it was $12,500 for 122 square meters."

The process went quickly and efficiently. Six months later, Bob returned to revisit his future home. "It was Thanksgiving week the same year. I took the red eye from Oakland, got to Leon [the nearest airport] at five-thirty in the morning. When I got there, [at his lot] it was about eight-thirty in the morning, and I counted eighteen people on the lot. The foundation was about knee-high out of the ground. I still remember exactly what I said. 'Oh, this is interesting!' I was standing outside myself observing how I was reacting to this." He had done nothing to set the construction in motion.

It seems ironic to be talking about it now. We are sitting in Bob's kitchen. Although he's nearly seventy, he's wearing running shorts and a damp tee shirt, having just returned from a run when I arrived. The room is small, as are the living room and bedroom and bath. The total square footage on this floor is slightly over 500. It is the second floor of a guest house on his property, and it is the size of a double garage. Below us is an office and powder room next to a single garage stall. The total living space is about 750 square feet. The main house has not been built, but Bob has no plans to go on.

The feeling around us is high tech, the appliances stainless steel and top of the line. The counters and floors are black polished concrete. All the ironwork, the stair rails, garage door and street door, are custom made. The architect's hand is in every detail. Bob awaits the time when Alan, his partner, can wrap things up in San Francisco and join him here.

He pauses for a moment, seeing himself standing at the edge of the other lot nearly five years before.

"I was surprised I was so calm and collected rather than going crazy. I immediately called Francisco, who had sold us that lot. I said, 'Do you know, somebody's building on that lot.'

"'Oh, no you're mistaken. It's not the right lot.'

"He was there within about ten or fifteen minutes. He confirmed that it was the lot. In the meantime Alan had put a down payment on the lot next door from the same guy. He put $3840 down. We had decided that at 122 square meters—I designed a house to fit that, but there was no yard and Alan wanted garden space, a yard, and maybe a little studio."

It made sense to go back to the *notario* who had handled the closing, but *notarios* don't do litigation, so Bob was referred to his nephew, who was an *abogado*. Two years of sorting through the details followed, in which Bob found that the seller of his lot had sold it again to a Canadian woman, who had immediately begun construction. She and her husband fought Bob's claim with the nastiest lawyer they could find in San Miguel. Furthermore, the name of the seller's sister was also on the property, and she hadn't signed off on either sale. To the nephew *abogado*, who had other interests, it didn't seem worth pursuing after a certain point.

"Well, I had all my money in that lot, and it became clear that this was not going to be cut and dried." Bob found a new attorney. "We ended up with a compromise. They got Alan's lot, without a foundation on it, so he lost his $3840. I kept possession of the lot with the foundation on it. I eventually was able to sell it to the woman next door who needed it for a parking lot." Bob got $15,000 for it. Why this didn't disillusion him? It seems like it would sour anyone on San Miguel and the pitfalls of doing business here.

"Even after that incident it didn't deter me at all. I was kind of amazed that I could stand outside myself and watch myself react."

I motion to the surrounding rooms, wondering how he could go from that disaster in the Independencia neighborhood to this. We are halfway across the city from that first misstep. "I still wanted to live here. I had been coming down three or four times a year hoping this would work out."

At the end he came across the architectural firm of Renfield, Fenster and Dilworth, (RFD) of Los Angeles. "I went through their website and there were all these fabulous modern buildings." Up to this point Bob had been thinking his house would be a colonial design, but he had been drawing house designs himself since he was fourteen—always in a modern idiom—and had always wanted to be an architect.

"We met with them and said we just wanted to build a *casita* because it would be five or six years till Alan was down here and we could build a bigger house. Then we'd use this for a guest house. I had cleared $137,000 for this project [from the Oakland condo], and I had a bit of an IRA, but not much. We had a very limited budget. We met with Ryan Dilworth, and he did preliminary drawings, concept drawings and worked out an agreement that we would pay RFD hourly for design work. We came up with about a thousand square feet for the first building. He told us $60 a square foot.

"Well, that sounded pretty damn good. We didn't have a lot yet, so I made that my primary business here.

On one visit in 2006 I saw forty-three pieces of property in ten days and narrowed it down to three. Ryan Dilworth was here at the same time, after I narrowed it down, and he looked with me. By far, he liked this one the best. The other one—I loved the view from San Rafael, but it was a very rough neighborhood, no paved streets. It would be definitely pioneering to be the only gringo in the neighborhood, no less to build something that stood out like a sore thumb. This lot here was 440 square meters, and four times more expensive than the first lot."

It had now been three years since the purchase of the original property. The owner of this one would only come down from $44,000 to $41,000, and the architect was pressuring Bob to get it at whatever cost. Bob and Alan came up with the money between them, only to discover there was a problem with the boundaries. Their neighbor to the left, who was the San Miguel director of public works, had two twelve-and-a-half meter lots, and measuring from his left boundary, his property ended two meters inside what Alan and Bob had just bought. The preliminary house drawings were already complete.

"We got into a legal thing with the owners on both sides. Who owes me two meters? It sounded almost like a replay of the Independencia property. That delayed the building here by about six months. Finally it turned out that the public works director was wrong. His property was two meters narrower than he thought it was. He admitted it. Once we were cleared, we started construction on October 2, 2006. It was supposed to be done in six months. It was finished at the end of September, 2007. I had moved down here on June 1, because I had sold my condo and was renting. I stayed with friends."

I ask the dreaded question; did the house come in on budget?

"Midway through Dilworth said, 'You know, I think steel is going up. It's part of China and the whole world economy.' Steel went up, and we bought a lot of steel ahead of time. This entire property has a deck, a concrete deck. Originally this house was designed to follow the contour of the land. It would have meant our [unbuilt] master bedroom would have been approximately fifteen or sixteen feet below street level, and the bathroom was at the very back. We got very concerned about sump pumps running all the time. San Miguel had power failures frequently, more so than now. We would be so far below the street level, we'd be pumping sewage all the time, constantly running. We're looking at the cost of electricity, so the buildings were the same but the elevations got totally changed."

Electric rates in San Miguel have three tiers. The lowest rate is extremely reasonable, but doesn't cover much usage. The second bracket is bigger, and the third covers all usage above the other two, but the cost per kilowatt hour is four times what it is in the lowest bracket. Bob's proposed sump system would have been expensive to operate and would have resulted in sewage backup through the sinks and toilets during power failures, which are inevitable here.

"The cost of bringing in fill to raise the lot to street level was enormous. It worked out at almost the same price to put a deck over it. We spent a ton of money on these perimeter walls and that deck. We resolved it with a 2200 square foot basement that we have no plans for. At that point Ryan Dilworth said, 'I think we should be thinking about $85 a square foot.'"

Bob, thinking of his $137,000 proceeds from the condo sale, thought this was still OK, although it reduced his reserves by $25,000. Even if the total cost went to $100,000, it would be survivable.

"Then the discrepancy comes in. How much was the deck, how much were these walls? That wasn't part of the thousand square feet. Nothing was ever said about that. We were just drained to the point where there's nothing left. By June, all the bills weren't paid. I'm starting to do the math. We're down to zero here, and we've got more bills to go.

"The total amount, and there's a little more, but at that point when I moved in it was something like $310,000 we had spent." This for a project originally budgeted at $60,000. Bob had spent the entire condo money. He had reduced his IRA to zero. Alan had contributed about $40,000.

"What do I have? I have no equity in the U.S. anymore. I have no savings. Everything is here, so I started looking for mortgage loans. There are a couple companies, GMAC and GE Capital, who are now loaning, but it's 10% interest and the closing costs were over $10,000. The cost was like $25,000 to get a loan for $70,000."

Bob's cousin advised him not to do it, but to look into personal loans instead. "What do I have for equity? I ended up taking a Citicorp signature loan for $20,000." The rate was 10% fixed, but with no closing costs. A friend who had a large credit line then offered him $45,000 at 7.76%, his cost. By finding a consulting client in the States Bob was able to make $1500 a month for payment on these two loans, but then he lost his client after a year.

Now he's making interest only payments and looking for another solution.

Naturally his relations with RFD Architects were terribly strained. Most of the design work had been developed between Bob and Ryan Dilworth. Alan was not able to get away from his business to spend the same kind of time on it. "I'm torn between being nice to them and just hating their guts for what they got us into. But I have to take responsibility that I didn't do the things Alan told me to do, like you've got to get cost estimates, and so on. It's Mexico, you can't do that. Their philosophy, and Ryan Dilworth will say it publicly, is that they want to take care of the Mexican worker."

I wonder aloud whether anything will ever be built on the rest of the lot, which appears to be about three-quarters of the property. "Who knows? Alan's equity in his house, once it's sold, may provide something. But why should we have a $300,000 guest house that nobody uses? This place has had one guest since it was built. Maybe we should consider taking this table out of the kitchen, making the living room the dining room and through the back doors add a living room and a bedroom."

The day after we had this conversation Bob was informed that after Alan's divorce settlement was complete there would be no equity left to distribute. The depressed real estate market and the expenses of the divorce would eat up everything.

"Through this crisis Alan has actually encouraged me to move back to the States, sell it and just give up on this. In the initial panic I said, OK, I know the market's not great now, let's see what I can do, so I did go to realtors, and the best they could offer was maybe $295,00 to start with, knowing that it's going to sell for 5 to 10% under that, less another 5% for commissions." Bob would walk away with $250,000 at most, less the $50,000 he owes on the two personal loans.

"Then you have $200,000. What can you do with that? One of my friends in the States said, 'You can move back, you'd have a nice nest egg to live on.' Not in the Bay Area, unless I'm going to have a very short life. Alan was saying, 'You could live in Stockton.' He sent me e-mails of foreclosure houses for $60,000, $70,000. Have you ever been to Stockton? It is in the middle of f-ing nowhere. It's in the Central Valley, where it gets to be 120 degrees. I'd be living in a 1940s two bedroom house, a dump.

"No social life. Alan said, 'Well, you can drive to the city, it's only an hour and a half.' Do you know what gas costs? I'd be someplace in the middle of nowhere, I'd know no one, with no culture. Living on social security, barely making it, with $200 or $300 a month air conditioning bills."

There is a pause while we both contemplate this. I ask Bob what the future looks like at this point. This has become a real estate story, and most of the threads I've taken up with the others have been abandoned. Bob's life has become *about* real estate. What he eats and wears and does for recreation is *determined* by real estate, and whatever purpose or focus his life had before is long lost, lost since the first purchase of the original lot in 2003.

"Well, I'm not going to give this up to live in a hell hole. I'm going to be selfish here. Alan and I had a dream together and it's going to work. *I* am going to make it work. I have seen that for two or three months now I can live on social security and make the minimum payments."

Bob has listed his place on a vacation rental site and booked two months already. He will move into the 250 square foot office space next to the garage stall on the lower level. There is a shower stall in the powder room there. He has just bought an inflatable mattress for $82. The two months rent will knock down the principle just a bit on his two loans.

"I can make it. There are too many great things here, I know too many great people that I wouldn't have up there. You don't meet people in the States like you meet here. All this culture here, it's inexpensive. I know how to manage money, very little money. I can get by on $800 a month. Once this is paid for I can save $500 a month. I can get by here fine. Great eating places, great entertainment, great movies. I have social stuff at least twice a week, a dinner or a party. I'm not going back."

I ask Bob what he would say to someone contemplating a move here.

"Well, here is one thing. I've had enough training in human potential programs that I know that if you want to do something, just do it. Declare you're going to do it, make it public, then set up the steps and take one at a time.

I wonder whether, for many people, fantasizing about doing something like this is mainly a way of giving themselves relief from things they don't like about their life as it is. "Well, I think it's mental masturbation. You think about it, but in your heart you know you don't have the guts to do it."

I ask if he has any regrets, expecting a few.

"Even if this crisis with the money had nailed me more, I would *never* go back. No way. In spite of it all, I'm happy here."

❁❁❁

Although it's a cautionary tale, I think this story belongs in the "more bang for the buck" file. Usually these are about people who come down to boost a middle class life into an upper middle class life by the addition of maids and gardeners, swimming pools and rooftop verandas. In this case Bob Fredericks came down to stretch his retirement money. He was going to boost himself out of the poverty he could see coming when he ran the numbers on a Bay Area retirement.

Although it included enough body blows to level a regiment, the story is not like any other I've heard here, nor does it contain the slightest whiff of defeat. In spite of counting every peso, Bob Fredericks got what he wanted. Going forward, I can only see it getting better.

CHAPTER 4

BEING PREPARED

If San Miguel has a suburb, it might be Los Frailes. Not quite a mile up the slope from the traffic circle where the Celaya road crosses the Dolores Hidalgo road, a tall arch invites the passer-by into a more parklike setting than you'll find in the rest of town. Inside, numerous small squares suggest small town America, but the architecture of the detached homes is more the flavor of Mexican modern of a generation back.

The neighborhood slopes gradually toward the reservoir and it is quiet--none of the underlying buzz and ruckus of traffic and animals so common in the center of town. The silence partly stems from the fact that many of these houses are second homes for Mexicans and Americans. The nearly 500 years of organic evolutionary chaos that shaped the rest of San Miguel is not in evidence here. Instead there is planning. The pocket plazas are dotted with mature pepper and jacaranda trees and palms. Listening hard, you hear only birds. Here retired petroleum engineer Ron Jackson and his Scottish wife Linda have settled into a modern house with long views over the reservoir.

As an engineer Ron tends to leave little to chance.

Two years before his retirement he began to search for a place to live. His main criteria were that it be cheaper and have a more livable climate than Houston.

"The Web made the search very easy and there were lot of places we could look at. Linda and I have both lived internationally. Norway, in the U.K., Peru, so we knew we could live overseas. We wanted to find a place that offered the most value for the money. We felt that Mexico was easy, it's close enough to drive back and forth, and San Miguel appeared on lots of radar scopes." In 2005 they made four exploratory trips starting in April. This was their homework.

"And then we heard about Chapala," says Linda in the broad Scottish accent that has survived her sojourn in the States, "and we went and checked that out, but came back here."

What was not quite right about Chapala—a lakeside community just south of Guadalajara?

"Well, we don't totally agree on that," adds Ron. "I enjoyed Chapala. Linda felt like it was a much older community, and not as sophisticated, I guess."

"It didn't offer the same entertainment," she says. "The restaurants were few and far between and they tended to close early. When I came down here, immediately there was an attraction. There was something about San Miguel, but with Lake Chapala and Ajijic, no. It was a wee bit too provincial for me."

I suggest that it also has the reputation of being a cheaper place to live than San Miguel, where real estate is priced much like in the U.S.

"Without a doubt," says Ron, "which is probably the reason we didn't totally agree on it. I was hunting for something a lot more reasonable than San Miguel, and at the end of the day we could probably live in the United States in a lot of places as cheap or cheaper than here, but we wouldn't have the same good weather." This is an issue for Ron, who was born in Louisiana and raised in Oklahoma. His tenure in Houston was connected to the oil industry.

After the exploratory trip they moved to San Miguel in March of 2006 and rented a house for a year. "I thought with the view here it just reminded me a wee bit of Scotland. It's only ten minutes from here to go to [*centro*]. I think we've got the best of both worlds."

But they had no Spanish yet. "Holidays in Spain, you know, that kind of Spanish, but no more."

At that time the housing market in Houston was still stable and their house sold in two weeks. "It was scary, it was so easy," continues Linda. "We had friends moving at the same time and they just kept bumping into walls." They had priced their house at market value and it sold for about 1/2 of 1% less than the offer price.

Ron still does some consulting for the company he worked for before retirement. "They know me very well and I know the company very well. It's easy to employ me.

"I try to work somewhere between thirty and sixty days a year. I made two trips this year, the year before I made four; I did Hungary, Turkmenistan, and west Africa. It really works well because I don't work in the States. I don't pay taxes on the money up to $80,000. That was another reason when we retired to live outside the Untied States."

What does this involve?

"In Turkmenistan I went in and negotiated most of the contracts. They were running short on people, it was time for the country manager to take a vacation, and I went in as acting country manager for 40 days. In west Africa it was campaign-type work. This last time was six weeks as country manager. I would sit in the customer's office and coordinate the work that was going on offshore."

I ask if this was managing drilling in progress.

"No, this was remedial work. The wells are already drilled and they're needing maintenance. The company I work for is a miniature Haliburton or Schlumberger. They have all the service lines that those two large companies have."

The rest of the year Ron and Linda are quite happy to be settled into San Miguel. Their research trips and experience of living abroad in other countries guaranteed there were few surprises. "We knew more before we got here," says Ron, "than a lot of people we've talked to who've been here six or eight months. It constantly amazes me how little some people know about the rules and regulations, about how to do this and how not to do that. How to set up a bank account. People move down here and they've read books on how to live in Mexico on $800 a month and they've never done any online banking or they're not Internet savvy."

I turn the conversation in the direction of what Mexico is or isn't, have they come toward something or left something?

"I had left Scotland in 1980," says Linda. "As Ron said, we moved all over. We've never had a problem fitting in anywhere. I don't know what it is about Mexico. San Miguel is a very comfortable city. The people are lovely, and that's what I love. You walk around the streets and everybody speaks to you. Not so much only the gringos, but the local people, all with smiles on their faces, and I've never been made to feel unwelcome.

"We've just come back from a trip to Europe, and I noticed it especially because in Europe people don't talk to you. Their heads are down and they march right on past. We were in France and Switzerland and I went home to Scotland for a week too."

"I think it's easier to fit in, here in Mexico," adds Ron. "I know it's much easier to fit here in San Miguel. I also think that if you went to Dolores [Hildalgo] or a medium sized town anywhere in Mexico you could fit in fairly well. I don't think you'd be made to feel unwelcome."

After two and a half years how do the Jacksons fit into the community? Some expatriates talk about the cocktail set (two-for-one martinis on Wednesdays at Harry's), and there's the culture set and the volunteer set. "I wouldn't disagree with that," says Ron. "Every one of those strata are there, and probably a couple more."

"We've really been busy getting this house together," says Linda, "so we haven't sought these things out yet. I just don't know, I'm playing it slow." It's not yet been a year since the house was "finished," a term in that Mexico has nuances of meaning, some of which can mean *not finished*. There's something in the way Linda talks about it that makes me think they hadn't planned to build it, but before I bring this up she's moved on.

"This is the start of the rest of my life. All these years I've had to do what other people wanted me to do. I've had to toe the line to a certain extent. I don't know how much longer I've got so I'm going to be pretty selfish about things. If I want to do something I'm going to do it. If I don't want to do something I won't."

This suddenly has a familiar ring to me. Is there an element of what Mexico *isn't* in her comment? A sense of escaping a long run of obligations? She agrees that she doesn't sense the same burden in Mexico.

"But I think," says Ron, "that the same thing would be true if we still lived in Houston."

"Well, in Houston we have family."

"I'm not trying to speak for you," says Ron, "but I think what you're saying is I want to do what I want to do. We've made our money and we've retired. We don't have any responsibilities, and we can do what we want to. I would not have had any different feelings if I was in Houston than what I have now."

"There's time for me to find my niche and the same with Ron. There are people here who do nothing but volunteer."

I suggest that it's possible to replicate your old life here, in terms of how busy you are, and even though some people occasionally find themselves doing just that, few would admit wanting that. But things often change soon after arrival. For example, the Jacksons had never planned to build a new house.

"When we first came down here," Ron says, "we looked at some rental homes. They had one for sale for $300,000 and you could rent it for $1,000 a month. I'm pretty good at math and I knew I could beat that, so we'd keep our money in investments and not worry about it. Once we were down here the market changed a little bit. Desirable, larger homes had gone up considerably. I was at the point where I wasn't going to move again. So we hunted for a lot to build on." Although they weren't forced into building, the owners of the house they were renting were returning, and building at that point looked like a better investment.

The house has come together well despite whatever dangling threads might remain from the construction process. The style is what the Jacksons call "Santa Fe." It has a contemporary look from the street, but nods to local color schemes by using pumpkin stucco.

Was building a good experience? I ask Ron.

"I'll never do it again. I don't mean here. I'll never build another house. It's the first home we ever built, and it was very stressful from trying to manage the process. You're doing things in a foreign language in a foreign country and you're not really sure of the legal process. We used a Mexican architect who speaks perfect English. This was his third home here; he had worked in the United States. He came recommended from a friend who is an architect in New York. We felt pretty comfortable with the architect."

I can't help asking if they came in on time.

"No, we didn't come in on time. It was within four months. I don't know whether it's cultural, but it's very hard, in my opinion, for some here to admit they've done it wrong."

"Nobody apologizes," says Linda.

"But we gave Luis every opportunity. We said, 'Look, Luis, here's our drop dead date. Are we going to have any problem making that date?' He said no, not at all. Well, there was never a chance in the world that we were going to make that. And he ran out of money on the house. We bid a flat rate. It's my understanding that the majority of the houses built down here are built on a cost plus basis. We had come to an agreement on a price. He couldn't complete it for that price, so we put in some additional money out of our pocket."

And how far off was it? I had heard some real horror stories.

"He was probably 10% off." Ron looks at Linda and she nods somewhat sadly. My reaction was that they had got about as close as it ever comes here both in time and money.

"Now, having said that," Ron continues, "we built this house for about $87 a square foot, to include house and land and furnishings, which is not bad. Luis had never built a house quite this big, so he just got caught up in it. Architects have a tendency—I've been told this—they build the house they want to and not necessarily the one you want to. So it just expanded."

The Jacksons feel that even being in the house less than a year they could sell it at a 20% profit. The market in San Miguel is not robust, but neither is it as soft as in the States. One reason is that mortgages are not common here and houses bought with cash are not forced onto the market by foreclosure.

"We didn't want to do it, but we did it and the cost overruns haven't impacted our style of living. The way the [stock] market has gone, maybe it was better to have the money in the house."

Settling into the house hasn't settled them into Mexican social circles much. "Our problem is we still don't know the language. That's our fault. We do plan to rectify that."

"As does every gringo down here," interjects Ron

with a grin.

"Our problem is we live out here, we go into town maybe twice a week, and everybody you mingle with are gringos."

I raise the point that their neighborhood, Los Frailes, is thought to contain more Mexicans than gringos. "Well, they're part-timers," says Linda. "This house here," she rises and points out the window, "he's trying to sell that. He's from Mexico City. We hardly see him. The people next door are a lot older and they're not friendly at all."

"I think 70% of the residents here are Mexicans," says Ron. "It's a 20-year-old complex."

"It's not," adds Linda, "that we're not friendly. It's that it's so difficult because we don't have the language. You're straining yourself. Our architect speaks English, our painter speaks English, our maid doesn't, so I try and converse."

"Linda's much better at that than I am. I'm going to have to get more immersed in it also. I think that it needs to be a goal, but it doesn't need to be the driving goal. The driving goal needs to be to enjoy yourself."

So they are serious about relaxing, but the biggest change in their lives comes more from a complete change of schedule, it seems, than Mexico itself. "We've changed from the fact that when I was working I'd be gone three or four months out of the year and when I was home I was gone at six o'clock in the morning to the office and it would be six or seven before I'd get back in the evening. We're now spending ten times more time together. [Then] Linda ran the house and I earned the money. Now we are trying decision making. What should we do and what should we not do on the house and in other areas. Do you agree?"

"We spend more time together now than we've done in our entire lives. We've been married twenty-seven years. That takes working out. I worked part time in Houston as a part time receptionist in an animal clinic. We only saw each other properly on Saturday and Sunday, and a couple of hours at night. I think you need to make your own lives for yourselves, because too much is too much. That's one of the things for this next year is finding out what I would like to do and does he want to do the same thing, or take up golf, or whatever. Or just go our little ways and come back in again."

But what is a day like now for the Jacksons? Linda considers this for a moment. "Well, some days, not a lot. Ron meets friends three or four times a week."

"I have coffee with a fairly eclectic group. Wayne Greenhaw is one of them. Some are permanent residents, some are part timers." I mention the fact that Wayne Greenhaw is a writer who won the Harper Lee Award in 2006 and is also a close friend of hers. "That three or four mornings a week enables me to keep my mind sharp and discuss various things that are going on in the world. Male interaction is one of the things I miss most."

Which leads me to wonder how close they stay in contact with events in the States.

"I'm not as good as Tom Brokaw," says Ron, "but I'm right behind him."

"He's on the computer all day," says Linda, who spends considerable time herself online keeping up with events in the UK. "And then we've met a lot of people down here whose company we enjoy, and so we go out a fair bit."

"And this has been a great house to entertain in," adds Ron.

I touch on the question of return to the States. Ron doesn't need to think about this for long. "If Mexico doesn't seem right for us a year or two from now. Maybe we get tired of Mexico and decide to move to Panama. Do I think that I'm going to die in Mexico? Probably not. Unless I'm dying tomorrow. Linda would like to go back to the UK or to Europe."

"If one could afford it," she says, "and one couldn't. But I love Europe. There's still so much to explore there. I lived twenty years in America and loved it, don't get me wrong. I just became a citizen two or three years ago. But I miss the UK. Although we were just back for a week and it poured with rain. I thought, I'm never coming back here. We love this weather."

"The United States," says Ron, "in my opinion, is the best country in the world to live in. But there are lots of other countries that are very nice to live in, especially when there's a termination date. When you know that you've been sent to Peru for three years. I was in Aberdeen for three years, I was in Norway for two years. If our investments were Euro-based, or the exchange rate suddenly flip-flopped, I would not be opposed to living in Europe...I did some work in Romania. It's such an unspoiled country—not in Bucharest, but outside of Bucharest it's beautiful. We looked at a lot of places."

"We could pretty much live wherever we wanted. Right now, we love San Miguel. Are we going to stay here another ten years? I don't know."

Where would they go if they did decide to leave?

"I think we'd probably look at Panama," says Ron. "It has some advantages. English is the primary language. Outside of the Canal Zone it's mountainous so there is less heat and humidity."

When I raise this issue of cultural activities in Panama both suggest that this concern is secondary. Linda confesses she's not a museum person and is not likely to spend time sitting in front of paintings, although she enjoys art. She acknowledges she's never been to the Louvre. Culture was not what brought them to San Miguel.

Feeling that their commitment to this place is not the same as some in these conversations, I ask what does not work for them here. A long silence follows.

"I don't know that there is anything," says Linda.

"Some of the bureaucracy," says Ron. "And the fact that nobody really knows, like when you're getting a building permit, you can talk to two or three different people. One of them will tell you this is how you do it, another something else. That type of bureaucracy irritates me. Other than that, I don't know. We've kind of gotten gringoized on this thing with Mega. The big box stores are here."

"One thing that does bother me," adds Linda. She goes on to describe a furniture order that was promised for before they went to Europe. When it didn't come she called and said leave it until we come back. Now she can't reach him. "And the fact that they'll never phone you to say, 'I know we had an appointment but I couldn't make it.' Three days later they'll show. We've been told that's part of Mexico. That's some of the downside for me."

Which leads me to ask what they might have done

differently.

"Building the house," says Ron immediately, "is one of the things we would have done differently. I would have done a better job of timing and controlling some costs."

I wonder aloud whether closer cost control was possible, having heard some horror stories.

"I'm not sure whether I could have or not. When I said we had a 10% overrun, the truth is that if I had gone to another architect, his prices would have been 15% higher so I might have saved myself a lot of heartache by demanding a more realistic timeline. We really didn't have any weather-related delays. We all think we can get it done better, but I didn't get it done better. There are some things about the house I would have changed. I'd have made it smaller."

"I think," adds Linda, "we've very lucky considering that there are a lot of horror stories out there. At the end of the day we've got a beautiful house."

As for what they might add that would clarify the picture of their experience here, Ron suggests, "We didn't have any great surprises because we did a lot of research. I think that many people fail to do that. They come down here with blinders on. They get lots of shocks about the cost of things. San Miguel is an expensive city, compared to the rest of Mexico. I could live in Houston as cheaply as I can right here. There's a lot of places you can live on four or five thousand dollars a month."

"We really like it here," says Linda. "We really do. I wish I could put my finger on it as to why I just think it's another little part of our path in life, and yet it's home."

CHAPTER 5

LEAVING IDENTITY BEHIND

Hicks is house is built on an uncleared cemetery. His youngest daughter disappeared headfirst through a TV screen sometime back. On sunny summer afternoons rotting corpses bob like apples in his swimming pool. Is it all in his mind? Absolutely, and there's more where that came from.

The mind in question is that of Hollywood producer and screenwriter Michael Grais, author of the screenplay for *Poltergeist*, his first big success. It was followed by *Poltergeist II* and eight other successful films. The unassuming and ironic Grais confesses to being sometimes too frightened to watch the films made from his own screenplays.

Jennifer Grais is a healer and former back-up singer for Jackson Browne. Many of her days are spent on the back of her white gelding, Solo, wandering the hilly trails and arroyos outside San Miguel. Connecting with nature is critically important for her.

The Grais' escape from Hollywood to San Miguel came by a road somewhat less well-traveled than most. They started by spending a month in India, unaware that going there opened a door that was an exit from their lives

53

in Los Angeles. It didn't take the entire month for them to realize they couldn't go back home in any permanent way.

When it was time to return to the States, says Jennifer, "we were ready to live somewhere else, we were fed up. Michael especially was really burned out in Los Angeles. He just felt like he couldn't escape Hollywood. Everybody thinks the same there. Even in this beautiful canyon [Topanga], a lot of the people are in the movie business. They'd ask, 'How far up the hill do you live?' It was that hierarchical. At first I thought they were really interested in where our house was, but I realized later they only wanted to assess how high up the hill we were." It was a metaphor for rank in the film community. "There really was no escape from that mindset. It was very isolating."

But while the trip to India initially held no suggestion of escape from Los Angeles, it did highlight some things that were missing from their lives. "The experience in India was very mind-expanding," says Michael. "We were with people from all over the world. I realized how much I missed communicating with people other than those who were talking about the latest film grosses or whatever the constant conversation is in Hollywood, which is only about money."

"Or about stars," adds Jennifer, "what actresses are doing."

"Or what Britney Spears is up to," he adds, "what underpants she's wearing."

"But it was amazing watching him in India. There were park benches and people would just gather around them and there would be somebody from Brazil or Africa. It was *so* stimulating, and he was so quiet and isolated in

Topanga Canyon on the hill. But there he was like the Godfather, entertaining on the park bench, cracking everybody up. When he came home from all that stimulation and camaraderie, that was when it just snapped for him." A serious look comes over her face; she is seeing it all. Again the turning point moment.

Michael nods, seeing it too. "And then I said, 'This is beautiful, but it's a beautiful cage,' and I can't live in it anymore. I said, 'We're moving, and I don't know where.'"

Jennifer surfed the Internet in search of a place that would restore their lives. "I was looking for a community that would be similar to what he had experienced [in India]."

She had not found the same lack of community in Los Angeles because she had never sought it in the same way. "I tend to isolate [myself]. As long as I'm in nature and have a few animals and can do some healing work I'm pretty fine. It was nurturing for me. It wasn't nurturing for Michael, and I wasn't in the business in the way he's in it, so I could withdraw."

No place in the States seemed right. Every place she looked at was either too far away from an airport, or too isolated in general. "I just couldn't find any place that seemed easy, was walkable, that would make life better." Friends had told them about San Miguel, knowing about Jennifer's love for old buildings and culture. They came down for a week to look at it, and they've been in San Miguel ever since, with brief interruptions to rent their Topanga Canyon house and arrange their move. "When we came here, it seemed to answer a lot of those questions," she says.

"Every place we looked, no matter where we looked" says Michael, "and we looked from the east coast to the west coast, [we found that] basically life in the States is the same everywhere. You live in a house, you get in your car, you drive to your office, you get back in your car, you drive back to your house, watch television, go to sleep, get up, and do it again. There's almost no city that's different; everything looks the same now."

Now they live in a city that *is* radically different. When he left Hollywood he had either produced or written the screenplay for ten successful films and had done extensive television work as well. Although he has recently offered a workshop in writing for films, Michael has moved away from screen writing himself to focus on two novels.

"The longer I'm here, the longer I'm away from that environment, the more comfortable I feel. And the more I realize how mentally enslaving it was being in that environment. It was incredibly limiting, just to be on top, to have a movie in production, to drive the right car, to live in the right house, to be at dinner with the right people, friends with the right people. You're always working."

One of the first things they discovered about San Miguel was that, while it was a fine place to work, it was not a place that was *about* working. While the Mexicans are a hard-working people, that virtue is not at the top of their list.

"We'll be here one year at a time until notified otherwise," says Michael. "It seemed magical. It was beautiful, the people were friendly, there was a large expatriate community here, so it made it easy to communicate with people. We just loved it. It was a walking city, I didn't have to drive. There wasn't a lot of pressure to do one thing or another."

"When we arrived I was struck by the flu," says Jennifer, "which usually means I'm moving through a pretty big transition, because I hardly ever get sick. I was in bed sleeping that off, and Michael was walking the city."

Moving about on foot was refreshingly foreign for him after driving everywhere in Los Angeles. Every trip had been a minimum of half an hour in the car, often much longer.

Grais now has the feeling of being in a creative atmosphere, but one of a much more relaxed kind than he was used to. "There's not the feeling that you're competing with everyone around you. There's no big Hollywood contingent here. No one cares where you live, how big your house is, because no one can tell where anyone's at, in that regard anyway. There are successful people living here in all kinds of strange environments." San Miguel is a town of inward looking houses, where the condition of the street walls often tells nothing about what a person might find inside, or who.

"We fell into a very eclectic and wonderful group of expats: writers, sculptors, painters. No one seemed pressured to do much of anything other than what they wanted to do." He looks at me as if to say how utterly strange that is. It's hard not to notice the recurrence of words like pressure, enslaving, limiting, competition, escape, burnout, mindset.

"The work ethic is the inverse of what it was in Los Angeles," Michael continues. "If you work too hard here, people wonder why. Coming to San Miguel was probably the first time in years that I didn't carry a cell phone. I haven't carried one since I've been here [thirteen months] except maybe twice. We can't figure out how to get the messages off it, we can't remember the number. You get to a point in your life where you've just had it with all that."

The move itself was not difficult once the decision was made. Within four days after returning from their one-week test visit they had leased out their California house for two years. Their furniture stayed with the house, so there was no moving issue that required a large truck. They brought their three cats by plane and made an additional trip to bring their car. Solo, the gelding, came in his own trailer.

"I'm learning dressage, and I ride trail," says Jennifer. "It's more about the connection for me. I've only been riding about four years." They find that the facilities for boarding and training are five times as good as in Topanga Canyon and the cost is about half.

The only way being here has differed from their expectations is that it is better. There has been a process of discovery, of coming across things that hadn't contributed to their decision to move here but nonetheless added to the experience. "It's continued to become deeper," says Michael, "on an interior level. I'm changing in a way that I don't think I could ever change in the United States. I just keep cutting my ties to all the things I grew up thinking I had to be. What you find here is that people are not trying to achieve greatness. They don't believe that not having money is any excuse for not having fun. Work is not a priority.

"If you looked at my life objectively it may have looked like an outsider kind of existence. My graduate school was in poetry. I wasn't on the corporate treadmill. I was on the *artistic* treadmill, which a lot of people don't think is a treadmill, but it is a treadmill. You're still trying to make money. What I discovered was that I even though I went to Hollywood to make movies and not to become a capitalist or to be on the materialistic treadmill, that's still what it is. Your work is determined by how much you make. It's not like you can make movies that don't make money and still keep working. The money came with it whether that's what you were seeking or not. That starts to become the value. You keep getting a bigger house, and a better car, and your expenses go up and it just keeps going on and on until you're trapped.

"It comes to the point," Michael says, "where you don't even know you're trapped, and you think you're having fun, but you can't sleep at night and you're alone. It's not fun and you've basically been brainwashed by the American Dream."

How did he get co-opted by this system?

"Once you're in it happens very fast. One day I was making nothing, and the next day I started working on an Emmy Award winning television show called Baretta, and making a lot of money every week."

Twenty-plus years after the show ended, the star, Robert Blake, stood trial himself on a murder charge and was acquitted. Michael and Jennifer both pause for an ironic laugh. "About the only psychopath in Hollywood I haven't worked for is O.J. Simpson," says Michael. More laughter.

Now, thirteen months after the move, it's easier for Michael Grais to get perspective on the Hollywood portion of his life. While *Poltergeist* was an enormous hit, it is not his personal favorite. None of his theatrical films are. The one he likes best is a television documentary called *Visitors from the Unknown.* "It was the first serious look at alien abduction and crop circles on network television where we weren't making fun of the people who were saying they had been abducted or seen a flying saucer or unidentified flying object. I'm very proud of that. I'm also proud of another television movie that I made for Showtime called *Who Killed Atlanta's Children?* which is a true story about the Atlanta child murders."

Meanwhile Jennifer is on another path, one that she had already followed in Los Angeles when she was in the music business. "I've always been a singer, that was my career, but while I was doing that and song writing I met this woman who was a healer, and she's on a path called shamanism. It's just seeing life in everything. It's very similar to the Eckart Tolle point of view that everything is alive, part of a divine presence. If you can move into that mindset, you can experience more joy and bring more of it to people who are ill. It's like a wholeness-balance thing. So she helped me a lot and she just became my teacher." Jennifer had gone through a period where she'd experienced a long series of bad dreams. The shamanist teacher brought rapid relief. "The work was really effective and so powerful for me that it just felt like home, like music always felt like home, and this particular healing path always felt like home."

"And the healing modality we learned in India," adds Michael, "Jennifer has incorporated into her shamanic work, and she and I do it as well. It's great fun and people have amazing reactions."

"It's completely compatible with the two paths,"

Jennifer says. "It's very shamanic what we're doing by giving a blessing sending loving energy to somebody. It's like *reiki* or like shamanism where you're bringing balance."

At the same time there was the music. She has toured with Jackson Browne, opened for Tom Petty. "I've been a singer in Los Angeles, doing session work, being a hired gun. That allowed me to make enough money to make a couple of records. The first record I made as a soloist got me noticed by some musicians who happened to be Jackson Browne's band, and so we all made a record together, without Jackson. Then when he needed a background singer, they recommended me."

Jennifer went on to record an album in a cave near Taos Mountain using some of the local Native American musicians. Once she had laid out an assortment of offerings in the cave, as her shamanic teacher had advised her, a swarm of bees arrived and surrounded her and the drummer and the microphones. She sang to them.

What do they do now? Jennifer has continued her healing work and is writing as well.

"This is a very active community here," says Michael. "From my point of view there's a lot of opportunities if you want them. But what I discovered early on is that if you sign up to do all the things that you can do here you're not doing anything different than what you were doing in the United States. I opted out pretty quickly."

They both realized that they had no desire to repeat their experience of California, nor did Michael want to work the way he did in Hollywood. He is now the only one who can impose pressure on himself.

Fitting into this society is a more complex matter. They don't find the wealth and poverty of San Miguel (and Mexico as a whole) greatly different from Los Angeles, but one difference is that where they lived, in Topanga Canyon, the poverty was not in view. "Unlike San Miguel," Michael says, "you don't walk through South Central LA, whereas you can walk through communities here where the homes are half built, or are shacks. You see that, and you see multi-million dollar homes. Some are the size of hotels that two people are living in. Personally, I don't feel that affected by it."

"The only thing I feel affected by," adds Jennifer, "is what you said earlier, that there's a huge community of Mexican people and I'm not part of that. I tend to isolate anyway. Unless I start volunteering at hospice or something, I'm probably not going to become a huge part of this community. What does affect me is that I feel like a perpetual visitor here. I'm conscious of being respectful, but I don't really belong here. I love the parades and I love the fiestas but it's not my party."

"I have the opposite reaction," says Michael. "I *like* not being at home here. I don't want to really be a part of the Mexican community. I don't feel welcomed into it. I don't think I've met four Mexicans who I want to know, and I don't care. That's not what I'm here for. I'm not here to become the savior of the Mexican people. As far as I'm concerned, they're saving *me* just by being who they are."

Jennifer isn't sure she would want to be more closely connected either. She has a clear view of where she stands. "This is not home. The parties, the architecture and the history that are so amazing, are not mine."

Could they get further into this society even if they wanted to? There is a carefully stratified class system in Mexico. There are few rags-to-riches stories. People don't strive to better their positions, they strive to improve their lives within their positions, recognizing that their social rank will always remain unchanged. Of what class are Americans who might wish to know them better? They may be economically similar to upper- middle class Mexicans, but they don't share the elaborate social graces that mark each stratum and therefore connections remain ambiguous, polite but not more than superficially connected.

"Unless I took the point of view of a student," says Jennifer, "it would be pretty tough to really get in here [to find a place within Mexican society]. In terms of volunteering and doing healing work, I give this blessing to people on the street, then it's all one. We're all connected and I can see in their eyes that they don't care what nationality I am. If I tried to put on feathers and jump into the Aztec dance, that would be inappropriate. But I agree with Michael. I'm not here to be a Mexican citizen. I'm just here to enjoy it and be a visitor and I'm going to be as respectful as I can."

"I've also lived in foreign countries apart from Mexico," says Michael. "I mentioned Peru, and I also lived off and on in Greece and Italy and Spain. What I found was, that in those cultures where I spent any time, the people really brought you in and wanted you to be a part of their culture, wanted to be friends with you, wanted to find out what you were like, and tell you what they were like. I don't find that to be the case here. I think that, as in the United States, where the Americans complain about the Mexican population, that they don't want to learn English, they don't want to intermingle, they want to stay among themselves, they don't want to be part of

American culture, and that's fine with me. "I find the same thing here. I don't think they'd really care if we all left tomorrow, besides financially. I think that a lot of them would be happy."

But he did not find this to be true in Peru where he was able to become closer to people. Part of the problem in Mexico is most likely the wretched history this country has with the U.S.

Does the lack of intimate and personal contact with Mexicans mean that Michael and Jennifer hold more firmly to their ties with the States? "It's diminishing," says Michael, "I keep up with the presidential politics, but not really with the day-to-day news. I think what's going on there is revolutionary, and so I'm fascinated with it at the same time that I'm horrified." He feels that the coming changes from the new administration, both politically and economically, will be dramatic.

"It's just the way I'm wired," says Jennifer. "I unplug from politics. I was like that back there. I just create my own reality. I'm interested in a bigger picture spiritually, and I'm glad I married Michael because he can keep me informed. Otherwise I won't listen to it; I won't turn on the news. I won't watch anything. I won't read the newspaper. We're heading, hopefully, towards a time of the possibility of a huge evolutionary leap. It's like we're heading towards bottoming out pretty quickly here. The earth changes and global warming—we have an opportunity to jump on this."

"I used to, when I was in the States," continues Michael, "watch the news and become depressed, enraged, upset, whatever. Here I watch it and because I'm not in the United States, because I have the barrier, I'm in a foreign country, I'm an expat, I don't get angry. I'm interested, but I don't become as obsessed or angry or depressed. I think I have a lot more objectivity about what's going on, and if it all falls apart, I'm never going back." He shrugs in a way that is not quite Mexican. Maybe that will come with time. This place invented the elaborate shrug.

Would Jennifer go back, other than for reasons of health or family? She feels it's a different answer than what Michael would give. "It's still home for me, and home as a concept is still comforting. I love my family and I love my friends. But in my mind where I live is so different from where Michael lives, and I deeply love *New* Mexico and I could go back there." She pauses to look at Michael. "But it would only be OK to go back if it's going back in a different way, for him especially."

"I really don't think anything is going to keep me there for very long," he responds. "I feel like I was a gypsy before I started on my career. I traveled all over the world and I loved it, and that's something Jennifer hasn't done before. This is the longest she's ever been outside of the United States in her life. I don't know that I'll live in Mexico for the rest of my life, but I don't see myself living in the United States for any length of time."

"It's not interesting anymore," she adds.

He agrees. "That, and the repression. On a day-to-day basis, it bores me. It's not attractive physically, nothings draws me into it. I see malls and highways; the homes all look alike. It just doesn't grab me. I'd rather disappear into the jungles of wherever than go back to that."

"It is a pervasive cultural mindset," Jennifer adds. "If there's a lot of people thinking about one thing, it's going to affect you. I feel it too when I go back there. There's a beauty thing that women get hit really hard with. There's an aging thing that people are absolutely obsessed with." It's hard to know how hard hit Jennifer is with it today. Now in her 40s, with little detectable make-up, her look is absolutely relaxed and in the right light, with her youthful features, she could pass for 30. Michael has just reached 60. His look is typically a bit grizzled, but he could easily be ten years younger himself.

"What's attractive to me about Mexico is maybe something that isn't attractive to Jennifer," says Michael. "It's that I don't know what they're thinking, so I can't be affected by it. They don't *let* me know the Mexican mind, and I don't care if I know the Mexican mind. I'm not here for them."

"There's a kind of freedom in not being an insider," says Jennifer. "There are certain doors that are closed, so you're like a voyeur. But I think people in general are so nice here, they are so alive here. Just the people working in *tiendas* [neighborhood stores]. That's the first thing I notice when I go back (home) is that people are dead... they're not there."

"One of the things we notice all the time," adds Michael, "is that if you're in the States and you're near children, you hear crying. There's crying all the time. Here I have heard crying *twice*, with all the kids in the streets here."

"And there's a playground back here and an entire school. I never hear them," says Jennifer.

"We have 500 kids in back of us. I haven't heard anyone cry. I think these people are great. I'm just not a part of it, and don't expect to be. Just being among them, just being here, walking down the street, you say *buenos dias*, they can't wait to say *buenos dias* back to you. There are people in the States you'd cross the street to get away from. I've never had that feeling here. I've never been afraid once; I've never had a lot of the negative feelings that I have in the States."

"I don't feel afraid here at all," adds Jennifer. "I just think in general there's an honor system, a natural respect that's really sweet."

"And if you don't want to say hello to anybody when you walk down the street, there's no bad feeling about it."

How about Mexican politics? The Graises are of a liberal mindset not unusual for their Hollywood background. The government on the federal level in Mexico is of a conservative bent that likes to dress up in revolutionary clothes. It's widely recognized as a charade. There is no likelihood that anyone with money here is going to be forced to share it. Even waves of revolution haven't changed that. There is a saying here that describes the outcome of every revolution: Same horse, new rider.

Michael's initial take is that the politics are an example of things he's excluded from. "The fact that there are more reporters murdered in Mexico than in probably any other country, that's a fact, but that's *their* fact. I did a lot of research on the Mexico-U.S. border for a screenplay on the drug situation. The Border Patrol versus the drug cartels and if you read the news you hear about all the gang wars that are happening on the Mexican side of the border over routes into the United States for the drugs. I got a really good look at what was going on in that world. I saw 2,000 Mexicans jump the border into the United

67

States on foot in one place in one night, so I've seen what's going on, and I see the corruption on both sides of the border. I also followed it up to see why it's happening. It's all part of a political plan. They never intend to close the border. The drugs are not going to be stopped and the cartels are going to flourish. One of the largest parts of the gross national product of Mexico is drugs. I wish the people of the United States didn't need so much drug use to cope because if there wasn't a market it would stop.

"We had a conversation with a tour guide we met," continues Michael, "who was very much of the theory that we stole California and all these states from them and they wanted them back. I said hell, you've already got them back. You're the largest population in all of California. What more do you want? And we're coming down here in droves! I think there's a pattern, and I could be wrong, but it seems to me, and maybe it's because we're here that we feel this way, but it feels like the tribes are shifting, and that people are moving all over the world."

"The same thing is happening with the Asian culture," adds Jennifer.

"I lived in Canada for years," says Michael, "and in Vancouver the population is half Chinese and half Canadian. It would not be even close to the interesting culture that it is without the Asian influence. What's also interesting is that they don't mix, the same way that you don't see a lot of Americans or Europeans mixing with Mexicans. In Vancouver there's not much mixing either. I think I saw maybe two mixed couples in the entire time I was there. They want to be with their own people and Canadians want to as well."

Jennifer sees other ways of intersecting. "In the

areas where we can [cross over], I want everybody to enjoy their own individuality, of course, but I'm hoping that
part of this evolutionary shift is going to put us more often on that oneness plane than on that separation plane.
Areas where we can do it now are with food. We're not
threatened by other people's cooking. We think it's great.
We want to taste their food, we share food with each other.
We don't say you shouldn't cook like that. We want to buy
the pottery, we want to know how they do it.

"Healing has some of those areas. Everybody
wants to feel good, so if you're going to bless somebody it
doesn't matter if it's the Virgin Mary or the ancient Aztec
god. If you feel better, and I'm helping you feel better,
we're all happy. So there are areas where we do achieve
that oneness where we don't threaten each other. We don't
try to change each other and we just enjoy it. I'm hoping
we can do that, there can be less of individual tribes fight-
ing each other. Let's just enjoy what everybody brings to
the table."

Michael often finds the telling detail in more
specific examples. "The street we're on is kind of a quiet
street. I'm inside working, I'm writing. I write for a few
hours and I really don't hear anything going on out there.
So I walk out to the Ancha, which is the main boulevard,
and this happened just a couple of weeks ago. I found
myself in the middle of a parade, and people were dressed
like super heroes, there were little girls dressed as pussy-
cats, there were people in religious outfits. I couldn't even
begin to tell you what the parade was about, but it was
joyous and I found myself dancing to the music on the
street up to the church. Where are we going to find that
in the United States? It's not going to happen. It gives me

a great deal of joy and it blows my mind. It just gives me freedom." He pauses to sum things up.

"You're doing a book about the expat experience, and a lot of the expats here are artists or writers. They're finding a way to finance their lives through whatever they're doing, and that has to be done on a computer or the written word or art. I have found that not being so cued in or attached to a cultural identity allows you a lot of mental freedom to create. I find creating here to be extremely easy. I sit down and start writing and it just goes. There aren't a lot of the mental blockages that I would have created for myself if I was back in the States."

One thread running through these conversations concerns whether people are here because of what Mexico is or what it isn't. Certainly the food, the fiestas, the climate and the spontaneous parades such as Michael found on the Ancha San Antonio are all part of what it is. But for the Graises it seems that greater weight might be placed on what it isn't. In this case, it isn't the movie colony in LA, it isn't the USA. It isn't the need to announce the gross of your last film or say how far up the Canyon you live. Is freedom then a negative thing, the simple absence of restraint or of other people's expectations? The absence of the kind of identity that makes it difficult to break out of a specific mindset?

Or is freedom another word for possibility? Maybe it's not freedom *from* so much as freedom *to*? And if it is, then perhaps Michael's story is after all more about what Mexico *is*, rather than what it isn't.

Jennifer's take, aiming at a higher and more unified view of things, is not as tied to place, positively or negatively. Her connection is based on healing, which as she suggests has no limitation of culture. The place where it occurs is mainly a backdrop, perhaps in soft focus, and the action takes place in the foreground, close up. Sometimes it's a laying on of hands.

CHAPTER 6

A HARDER LIFE

Hearing about Renee Courtney's life in New York makes it seem so dense, so packed with explosive angst that her trajectory to San Miguel was much like that of a planet spun off the equator of the sun: explosive and inevitable.

We are sitting in her studio in a white stucco building on Cinco de Mayo, a sloping, busy cobblestone street on the south side of San Miguel. Around a small courtyard are several other shops. Up the block is the local *tortilleria*, where for the peso equivalent of 35 cents American you can get half a kilo of fresh warm tortillas wrapped in damp paper. The smell makes your mouth water. Across the street is a pet food store fronted by cages of parrots that eye you curiously as you pass. Four times a day the street is clotted with hoards of uniformed students. Three schools line the street further up, each working in two shifts. Attendance is not required after sixth grade. Some kids still manage to come, others don't.

"I grew up as a child actress in New York, and went to art school [studying jewelry] when I was seventeen through nineteen. I got away from that when my parents were getting a divorce. During that time I started working for the [talent] manager who had represented me in my career." This was after 350 commercials and three years on *Sesame Street*.

She probably tried out for *Annie*, I'm thinking. Renee's a strawberry blonde; with a pale complexion. She has a kind of in-your-face charm, keeping the frank determination of the New Yorker, but it's as if the abrasive quality of many people in the Big Apple has been gently rubbed away during her time here. She hurries on, tracing the thread that brought her to San Miguel, where it unraveled, like most things do that are too tightly wound.

"Later I opened my own talent agency, representing children for fifteen years. After getting burned out and experiencing the death of my brother, I was reconsidering life choices, saying, Do I want to sit here and do this the rest of my life? Or do I want to go back and do my jewelry?"

Renee spent some time in the research library of the Fashion Institute of Technology, where she had studied. She was not yet looking for a new place to live, only trying to see whether jewelry making could be a viable career change. "I was investigating options of where to study, where to go, where to work, how did I want to do it. In researching these possibilities, before closing my agency, I was looking at the artists' work I liked, and then I would read the article. Two of them mentioned the Instituto Allende in San Miguel. I had always vacationed in Mexico, on the beaches, because I loved it here."

She put the Instituto information in a file, not knowing when her life would allow her to connect with it again. "Two days later I went to a cocktail party. A girl friend of mine came up and said, 'Hey Renee, you go to

Mexico all the time. My mom just bought a house in San Miguel de Allende.'

"I thought, three mentions in less than three days. I went home and mailed away for a brochure. Later, when I decided to close my business, I was exhausted and strung out. I decided to take a break." A friend suggested she take a jewelry class in San Miguel. She came to San Miguel, checked out the Instituto Allende and met the jewelry teacher. The rest of her visit was spent getting a sense of the city. Back in New York she mulled it over for a few months. Then she reached a decision.

"Six months later I put everything in storage, sublet my apartment, and decided to come to San Miguel for six months to learn to speak a little Spanish, to take jewelry classes and get back into soldering and the real hands-on business of making jewelry. I came in January and four days later I met my husband to be in the *jardin*. At that time San Miguel was not the place it is today. You couldn't get a cup of coffee to go, there was no Internet. Very few people had television. This was about sixteen years ago."

Renee fell in love, with the town and with the Mexican gardener named Salvador who she met in the plaza. But there was a problem. "I couldn't see myself going from making six figures in New York to coming here and having nothing. I went home and started working in the jewelry industry. Two years later I came back for another six months."

I wonder aloud whether the Mexican gardener is waiting for her in the corner of the *jardin* during this hiatus. Four years pass. Renee moved to Denver and opened a jewelry studio while she studied with her mentor, master goldsmith Reno Carrollo. From him she learned not only the skills of making jewelry, but also operating a custom jewelry studio as a business. "That was where I really came to terms with what kind of jewelry I wanted to do, where I wanted to go with it. I was working other part time jobs, so I opened a studio and started doing repair and production work. I worked for him and other jewelers in my studio. God, I worked sixteen hours a day, every day of the week. I was also working with a therapist trying to figure out what I was going to do with this relationship and how I was going to get back to Mexico."

During this time she took another job as well, one that paid a salary, and started salting money away for her move. It seemed to her during this period that San Miguel was evolving into a more sophisticated place, and that more of her friends were coming down here. "*Conde Nast* had put it on the list of the ten best places to retire. Things were happening."

A year and a half passed, and Renee received a call saying that a jeweler she knew in San Miguel needed a manager for her shop. This was in 1999, and it finally pulled everything together. She had a now-or-never kind of feeling about it. After thinking about it so long it needed to become real. She came and started managing the studio, renting out space to traveling craftsmen.

"It was pretty mellow for a couple of years. More and more tourists started coming down. A lot of people would come for the winters and the summers. More Mexicans started coming in. Young families were coming, teachers on sabbatical brought their families for a year. After three months the magic would hit, and they had to figure out how to stay.

"One of the dilemmas of being here is that you can't just go and get a job. You have to generate your own income. They want to know you can pay your taxes and contribute something in order to stay here." For Renee, this was not difficult, but for others she knows who have tried it for six to eighteen months, there have been many failures, and people have gone back to the States.

"I was a successful businesswoman in New York, so I knew how to run a business." She found that in spite of being in a different country, most of the things that worked in Manhattan worked as well in San Miguel.

"After I was here a year, my husband and I got married, and two weeks later I got pregnant."

What developed was a simple, improvisational lifestyle. She began to understand the rhythm of the tourist trade, how to pace expenditures to match variable income. Her husband worked mainly as a gardener but also helped her in the studio. Gone was the six-figure income from New York, but gone as well was the New York lifestyle that required it.

Looking around the studio I see that one corner is for display, with cases and wall hangings for finished products. The rest of the space is taken up with tables stacked with trays of materials, beads, wire, tools and other things that make no sense unless they're on someone's neck or wrist.

"I was one of those quintessential New Yorkers. My friends said, 'You leave New York and in six months you'll be back, guaranteed.' I still think about New York, and I miss a lot of things about it, but I'll live longer being here. It's simpler, it's not as crazy and pretentious. I think in the United States there's this consumer-driven society now where you have to have the big house. You're working all your life to pay your bills and have these things. I personally was not finding that it was feeding my soul."

When the decision was made her family was shocked, believing she was too much a committed New Yorker to ever leave. "In the beginning you missed the availability of certain things: Heinz Ketchup, your favorite shampoo, peanut butter. You used to go and do something and what would take you five, ten minutes on the phone in the States would take three hours, two bus trips, an hour and a half on line, and then having the office close and having to come back after *siesta*."

"What is the trade off?" I ask. The answer varies widely in these conversations.

"One of my favorite things about San Miguel is the beautiful quality of light, and the weather. The fact that you are not rushing to do everything at such a pace and with so much pressure. The people here are extremely friendly. They take their time, and they live in the moment. There is a festival or fiesta almost every day here. If you're retired and you have time to enjoy all that, it's a little easier, but it gets in the way of doing business and moving things forward.

"If someone says I'll have this for you Tuesday, and then you don't have it Tuesday, and they haven't paid their phone bill and they don't answer their phone and you have to go find them and they're not there because they just decided not to come to work—there are many cultural things to get used to and expect." Renee has been able to make the required shifts in her expectations. Time management is completely different than in New York. It's more connected to expectations management. Being married to a Mexican man has also given her a view of how involvement with the local community works that is different from that of others.

"There are many different types of Mexicans. Mexico is very traditional--they don't want to change anything, they've been doing it this way for thousands of years. They are not motivated to be time-efficient. Or to make money [Renee laughs ironically.] I think a lot of that intimidates them. They're very private people, both among themselves and to Americans. There are people who will say hello to you, but you'll never get to know anything personal about them."

Renee believes that the existence of both formal and informal ways of saying "you" in the language facilitates a structure that fosters more rigid social divisions. "It's very rare that they will take you in and tell you intimate details of their lives. They weren't socialized that way. There's a much more formal face, almost a mask, that most of them wear, and it takes a while, depending on their trust level and how they feel about you, if they want to bring you in. Once you are invited into what I call the inner circle, you are almost treated like another family member. And you're expected to behave that way."

Being married to a Mexican man has placed Renee within this circle, but she has worked on this and relationships with Mexican friends as well. I ask whether there is socializing together with both U.S. and Mexican friends.

"My life separates out three ways. There's the American group, the pure Mexican group, and then there's the group that *is* mixed. There are a lot of Mexicans here that have never been out of San Miguel or the state of Querétaro or out of Mexico. They haven't been to America to experience what the culture is like. Then we have a group of parents at the school we go to who are very committed to having their children be bilingual, to know Americans, to have their children break out of that old traditional thing."

Renee's daughter, Chelsea, is fully integrated into this bilingual school, but Renee recognizes disturbing elements in the culture. "There is a much different treatment of women here; they're very far behind. I am a child of the sixties. My mother was a proactive feminist and raised me to be independent, to believe the world was mine, that I could do anything a man could do except father a child. Now I'm forty-seven. I grew up with that, and I was placed in situations all my life where I had opportunities I could take regardless [of my gender]. "I work with baby sitters and housekeepers who are completely controlled by their husbands. They have no education, they follow the strict Catholic values of the family and the social structure here, and they know their lives are not going to change. They accept it and they move through it. I have a daughter who's going to be, I hope, a lot more like me. It'll be interesting when she gets to be dating age and we'll see what happens."

Will Chelsea, I wonder aloud, find a smooth fit in this culture? Will she possibly, with a Mexican look and a New York attitude, be found uppity in San Miguel? An old fashioned word, but one, I think, that has the right nuance for this *machismo*-dominated society.

"Well, you'd have to meet Chelsea. I don't think she'd ever be thought of as uppity. She's way too charming for that. Then there's the conversation of the class structure that exists here. You're broken down by whether

you're from the *rancho* or the *campo*, if you have an education, the color of your skin, how much money you have,
social standing within the community, where you're from--
that's where the prejudices here come about. Some people
really embrace the Americans here, others would prefer
that we all just leave and go home.

"We go to the 'uppity' private school in town,
where a lot of the wealthy children go. They will never
have to work a day in their lives. It is the best education
possibility in San Miguel. It is truly bilingual: she can
speak, read and write Spanish and English, backwards
and forwards, without skipping a beat."

Talk of Chelsea's school raises one of the background issues of these conversations, the extremes of
wealth and poverty in San Miguel. Being from New York,
this is a familiar story for Renee. Chelsea, at age seven,
is sorting these things out as well with her classmates.
"Last year she came home one day and said, 'What does
it mean, my American mommy?' So, already now there is
the difference of Mexicans, Americans, *gringos*, *gringas*.

I hope to get to go to the States with her and have
her live there in her teenage years so she understands what
being an American really is as well, so that she's truly bicultural. A lot of the reception we get sometimes is not so
positive. People make immediate assumptions about me
because I'm so blond. I get special pricing everywhere I
go. I'm charged more at the markets."

Renee also has a sense that because there is a
substantial group of wealthy Americans in San Miguel,
businesses tend to focus on that end of the market. She
feels that she does all right, but has no place in the upper
income group. She has rented since she moved here, and

only recently have she and Salvador bought land in the La Lejona neighborhood with an eye to building a home. This is an affordable, up-and-coming area with a lot of construction already underway, and it's less than a mile from her studio. This sounds like a new level of settling in after nine years.

"I came and I made a choice in my life that works for me. I didn't leave the United States because I didn't like the politics there, or anything else. I came, I had an adventure, I fell madly in love with a man and a place where I could do what I love."

She does not follow the news from the States very closely, wishing she had more time. Mexican politics she sees more of, finding a sense of hope has come in since the election of Vicente Fox in 2000. "Mexico always reminded me of America in the 1950s. I don't know if the women will have the revolution women had in the States. I try to encourage these women and open their minds and talk to them."

Returning to the States, except for visits, is not on her map at this point. Until a recent trip she had not been back for more than three years. She was happy to get back to Mexico. Yet she views this issue in the light of what is working at the moment. Currently the answer is not the U.S., but she's not prepared to say this would never change.

"I used to have my life planned out. I'm taking a much different route now. We take it three to six months at a time, season by season business-wise. Things are changing. I am changing, my daughter is changing, San Miguel is changing. It's all changing so quickly that the best skill to have is to go with the changes, to find out what works best in your life and what doesn't."

This remark piques my curiosity. What *doesn't* work in this cobblestone and adobe paradise? She pauses for a moment. "The lack of true honesty. They'll say what you want to hear instead of what you really need to know. For me that is very, very hard because honesty and my truth and my reality are very important to me."

I wonder whether this is nothing more than *cortesia*, the Mexican style of politeness that places the desire not to disappoint, or to never admit not knowing the answer to a question, on a higher level than telling the truth. This can be nothing but frustrating if you're traveling and stop to ask directions.

"They do it with a different sense of conscience. They don't think it's a bad thing to do that. To find the real truth costs time and energy and emotion, and that is probably my biggest pet peeve." She gives me a steely look. "Cut to the chase. I'm a New Yorker; I'm an honest person. If I ask you a question, yes or no, whether I like it or don't, you're not going to hurt my feelings. I'm not a baby, I'm an adult. Let's get to the bottom line of it and move on. They don't move that way at all. That's very frustrating.

"It's hard to set up an intimate relationship knowing that they're not being real and honest with you. So [because of that] there are more acquaintances versus true friends or people you're having an intimate connection with."

I get the sense from this conversation that Renee Courtney has gotten into the Mexican culture more than most. Does she sense that she is different from other Americans here?

"Very much so, but I'm different than most people I know everywhere. In New York there was an embracing in that community of, 'if that's want you want to be, be your true self, be different, be unique.' Yes, I'm very different here, but I kind of like that. It was difficult in the beginning because I did try to integrate and be like the Mexicans. That didn't really work."

She was left with an absence of role models. Most Americans here are older and retired. Few think of starting businesses. Only in the last few years have other women of Renee's age appeared, some with children. For the first time she has peers.

But even after nine years some people at home persist in viewing her move as temporary. "They still don't quite have the understanding, and frequently people ask me when I'm going to move back to the States. I think a lot of people have the tendency to let their surroundings define who and what they are and give them their happiness. Mine is internal. I guess it has less pressure, less stress, more time, more space. I've been able to connect with myself, to create a completely different kind of life and fill a hole I didn't even know was there. It took about eight years of process to really make the change complete and to get solidified in the life I have now.

"One of the things I've realized here is that it is in many ways, a harder life. You have to work a lot harder here for the basics. The waiting on lines. My husband does a lot of that for me, so I can sit and work."

CHAPTER 7

THE ELECTRICITY GOES OFF AT TEN

I knew it was going to be good conversation when Betty Kempe greeted me at the door with a pitcher of tequila sours, a bottle of red and a bottle of white wine, and then introduced me to her parrot. Perched on the sill of the open door of her tall, cylindrical cage, the iridescent green bird cocked her head and regarded me with a golden eye.

"She's just showing off now, but she loves to have people talking around her," Betty says as we settle into the arcaded patio of her eighteenth century home. It sits high on Chorro, well up the eastern slope of the basin that holds San Miguel. The old casa surrounds us on three sides, and the view down the slope of her property focuses on her stone guesthouse, freestanding with a narrow staircase climbing one side. The garden, filled with gnarly trees and flowering vines, seems as ancient as the house.

"It's really more like a guest tower," she says.

Betty, now in her mid-eighties, goes back fifty years in San Miguel. As will sometimes happen, this bright place in her life began with a tragedy, when she was widowed in her 30s.

"How did you come to Mexico?" she repeats.

"Having a hotel and meeting all those people, I've had that question flung at me I can't tell you how many thousand times. You can imagine!"

I nod and pour us both a glass of wine, red for me, white for her.

"I was married with three small children, the oldest was ten, when their father died in an automobile accident. When I was a widow, living in Fort Worth, I had a friend who was going to drive and explore Mexico. Although she knew Mexico very well, I didn't. I'd never been anywhere except the border towns. This was about 1958 when I did get to Mexico [with the friend]. Like everybody does, you just absolutely swoon, and you've got to live here.

"So I came back the next summer to San Miguel. People ask me, how did you know about San Miguel? You can just imagine what it was like then. They were beginning to have GIs come down to study, and the art school had started. I had met someone who had been down here for a month, and she said, 'You will love San Miguel, and your children will like it too because there are hot springs pools and other kids there.'

"So we came down, and this is what really gets to people, I was going to rent a house or an apartment to be here a month. The Instituto Hotel, which I guess was the best hotel in town, was built right on the grounds of the art school. It was the magnificent price of five dollars a day with three meals. We stayed there while we all went to school. I studied art and history and Spanish with a delightful and charming refugee from Spain named Dr. Osino."

In those days the Instituto Allende that Betty

speaks of was under the leadership of its legendary found-
er, Stirling Dickinson. He had come to San Miguel much
earlier as a young man with considerable resources at his
disposal and bought the vast, decrepit building on Ancha
de San Antonio. It was once the hacienda of the Canal
family, whose former principal mansion still faces the *jardin*, the central plaza, and now furnishes quarters to Bana-
mex.

Thinking of the large number of courses offered
then, and the highly skilled staff that taught them, she
feels that both the quality of instruction and the range of
courses offered have stumbled badly over the years.

"Anyway," she concludes, "when we got to San
Miguel, that was the beginning. If you have a place in
your life when everything changes, that was it for me."
This makes me think for a moment. Certainly the death
of her husband was such a place in her life too, but that
was more a time of things coming abruptly to an end. This
time of arrival in San Miguel was a place where doors
were opening. It seems characteristic of Betty Kempe that
the second change, the positive change, is the more significant of the two.

Returning to San Miguel full time was only possible because a woman named Augusta ran a fine school
for English speaking children, and when Betty returned
after renting out her house in Fort Worth, the two older
girls were enrolled. It was 1959, and it was in the context
of this school that Betty and her daughters met Linton
Pitluga, a 15-year-old from New York State that we meet
in another narrative. The two live about a mile from each
other now.

Recalling this period brings up another thought.

"If I were writing about what San Miguel has been through in the way of changes and why all the old timers like me complain about the changes here, it's not just the money, it's not just that it was this wonderful, romantic place. There were fewer than a hundred non-Mexicans here, and now there are 5,000. Now that already tells you a lot about what has happened to life In San Miguel. The electricity used to go off at ten at night." What would happen to the refrigerator? Betty can't recall. Maybe they didn't have one. Maybe they were powered by ice.

"We all had oil lamps in our houses. There were no telephones, although I'm sure the doctors must have had them, and there was a telephone office. That office is now—I hate to say this, it makes me want to throw up— the telephone office is now Starbucks. Across the street was the San Francisco Hotel. Anyone calling would call the main number for San Miguel. This is how I received long distance calls. A little boy on a bicycle came to the house and would say, 'You have a long distance call from Fort Worth, Texas.'" She would jump in her car and rush down to the *jardin*, knowing it would take a while for them to reconnect the call. "In those days you could park any- where. There were more burros than cars. I would pay a little kid on the street two or three pesos to let me know when the call came, and I'd go over to the San Francisco Hotel and have a margarita and wait for my call."

When Betty relocated here the year following that first month-long visit, there wasn't much to adjust to. Her expectations were close to accurate, and she already knew many of the local Americans. The differences between then and now are in sharper focus.

"Not only did we have extremely interesting,

bright, and creative people in the way of artists and writers and people who had been in theater," but the media they represented were more diverse. Just as importantly, she adds, "You met them all. We have talented people here now, people I'd like to get to know, but we've got 5,000 [expatriates]. How am I ever going to get to know them? You don't. You just don't meet them because they come here and stay just a month or so. I used to stop people on the street if I saw them more than once and say, 'Are you living here now?'"

There is, of course, more of everything, even if the quality does not always measure up to what it was before. "As far as art exhibits, there were at least five or six a month. Now there are probably six a night, but this is what it was [culturally]. It was the kind of people you met; it was the kind of activities you were exposed to. You could walk to anything you wanted."

How did Betty get by during those early years? The Mexican government had much more stringent laws on the books about foreigners working. "No one could work at a job of the kind that you'd find it easy to get in the States. The only people they were interested in having come in here were teachers in a special field that Mexico needed."

As a widow she had social security for herself and the children and some insurance money. This provided about $500 a month—with three children. There was also rental income from the house she owned back in Fort Worth. "We lived very economically, and where else could you live that way?"

Eventually she married a writer and moved to Europe for several years. Later they lived in Chicago for five years, and after getting divorced, Betty, who knew French, took the girls to Switzerland and studied hotel management while they lived in Geneva. She already had a plan; she had never stopped thinking about Mexico.

"The hotel in San Miguel opened on Christmas Day 1969. The Villa Santa Monica was a wonderful old colonial building that had belonged in years past to a Spanish baron who was a silver miner, and then for a hundred years sat there empty." Later the property had been purchased by Jose Mojica, an operatic tenor who had begun a hugely successful film career in 1919. (I'm intrigued by the thought that films were all silent during this period. But Mojica was a stunningly handsome man, and perhaps the moviegoers just imagined the sound of his voice.) In 1947 he joined a religious order and moved to Peru, first becoming a monk and then a priest. He lived in quarters attached to the ancient cathedral in Lima. Involvement in the restoration of a school that had been destroyed by an earthquake led him to write his autobiography and return to film making to raise funds. In 1969 he returned briefly to San Miguel to celebrate the fiftieth anniversary of his film career. It was during this visit that he encountered Betty painting over a mural he himself had painted in the former bedroom of his mother, but I'm getting ahead of myself.

After school in Switzerland, Betty returned to San Miguel and looked for a suitable property. "I could have bought the Villa Jacaranda for $45,000. I could have bought a building behind the cathedral that is now divided into shops. That building was huge; it covered the whole corner and had been the bishop's palace. It was $23,000. Do you know why I didn't buy it? Because I had a very good lawyer, and he said, 'Having been a bishop's palace, if the government ever wanted to take it away, they'd just take it from you.'"

Finally she purchased the Villa Santa Monica from Jose Mojica for $55,000. "Mojica had done a lot of restoration and lived in it for years before he left to join his religious order." But then came years of rental between 1947 and 1969 when rooms were rented cheaply to students at the Instituto, and at times the building was empty.

"I was in the middle of remodeling and everything else we had to do to open a hotel and workmen all over the place, you can imagine what it looked like, and one of the workmen came to me and said, '*Señora*, there's somebody that wants to see you at the door.' He didn't know who it was. "I said, well I'm sorry but I'm busy now, tell him to come in here. It was Mojica. And Mojica comes in the front door and turns to the left, where guess what? I am putting finishing touches on a fresco he painted fifty years ago. The room was all done with a soft gold and white tone. I decided that the violent red and the violent yellow colors that he used were [too brilliant]. I had already learned about how to do this antiquing.

"So here I was up there with this antiquing—I didn't really change the picture at all--but just in the very brilliant colors. It's the first time in my life, I still brag about this, that I ever did something that just came to me in a flash, and it was the right thing to say when the artist himself walked in. "I said, 'Oh, Father, I'm so glad you came because, you know, I have loved this room—it was his mother's room—and this is going to be our biggest and most glamorous room. I only wanted to tone down these colors a bit, and I wonder if you could show me how?'

He got up on the ladder and showed me how to do the antiquing!"

Betty operated the hotel for fifteen years, selling it in 1985. It's one of my favorite spots in San Miguel still. We used to stay there on some of our visits, unknowingly occupying Mojica's mother's room, and we come for lunches now, just for the unequaled charm of the courtyard. I've used it as a background in my fiction three or four times. Betty's own parrot reminded me of the bickering ones under the overhang there when I came in.

It is still a unique institution and I ask her why she had sold it. "One person, running a place like that without any family—my children offered to help me but I refused to let them, because they had their own lives. I got to the point where I would have nightmares. There would be something like a crowd of people forcing me back through the dining room, out past the French doors, out to where the ravine is. I couldn't get away from them, and I said, 'That does it.' That told me I have seen too many people, had too much personal contact. I've worked too hard alone without anybody to spell me. It was a repeating dream. It reaches a point where you've been *peopled* to death." OK, that's clear enough. Betty is not vague about her reasons for quitting. Jose Mojica had died in 1974, so he would not be second-guessing her.

"When I sold it in 1985 I spent a year just looking for what I wanted to live in next, and this was it. Then it took another year to remodel it. I was just determined that I was going to have a colonial house I could remodel with my own feeling in it."

When the house was finished, she did volunteer work at the hospital, took more painting lessons, and

91

traveled again, something the hotel had severely limited for fifteen years. There were many trips to Guatemala, where one daughter lives, others to Santa Fe. Now, with a new hip and some difficulty with stairs, she doesn't travel nearly as much.

Betty and her brother inherited an old plantation house with fifteen acres outside of Natchez, Mississippi, but she does not get up there much now. At one time, she says, her grandfather owned thirty-two plantation houses in the area, including one called Sligo and another called Woodstock. Being a landowner in the States does not make her interested in the news or politics. She mainly watches on TV things that amuse her.

Her social life has come to include Mexicans over the years. "Even from the beginning, when there were only a hundred foreigners, what did you have to do? You saw your foreign friends. If your Spanish was not great, you didn't have Mexican friends. But through the years I would be pretty stupid if I hadn't made Mexican friends. On the other hand, except for the few that I have had for so many years, that just are friends like you are with your American friends, we don't socially combine like the Americans with the Americans and the Mexicans with Mexicans. But I don't know any Americans who have lived here as long as I have who don't have some Mexican friends. "You think of them as friends, you have them over for lunch, but it's not the same blending."

I ask her if she knew why there was always that slight hurdle that interfered. "When you live in a community that has one group of people who are obviously the wealthier, the better educated, it determines what kind of social life you have."

Betty's social life included Linton Pitluga's father, with whom she used to golf. When Linton and Phyllis came back to San Miguel in the 80s for a visit, Betty hadn't seen him since he was fifteen.

We talk for a while about the pyramid, a site about to open in a year or so. It's approximately twenty miles outside San Miguel on an unmarked piece of private property. Some years ago it was purchased by an English woman with an amateur interest in archaeology. The Mexican government had expressed no interest in it until that time. Now the antiquities office, INA, is in the midst of creating access to it. I knew that Phyllis Pitluga had been involved in mentoring a young woman archaeologist on the astronomical aspects of it.

Betty had said earlier to me she was sometimes vague about the years because there had been so many of them. I ask her how she feels about having spent half her life in Mexico. "I feel like one of the luckiest people in the world," she says. "I've had an extremely interesting life, I've met people from all over the world."

She patterned her life in San Miguel after Fleda McFarlane, who had turned her spacious house on Sollano into a hotel after her husband died. When people asked Fleda to dinner, her house guests came too. Her home had the sense of an ongoing house party, a feeling Betty tried to carry on at the Villa Santa Monica.

I suggest that Mexico is one of the few places she could have done that, it would have been much tougher in the States. "Oh, where *would* you do that in the States? Just tell me where you would go, where another language was spoken, where the historical background went back for a thousand years, and where you could have something that remained in the past. Only one place—think about it. Think about the U.S.A. as a whole and think about where you would go if you were a woman and you were thinking about opening a hotel where there would be some history and interest to the place. There aren't many places like that, but one of them is Williamsburg."

I admit she has a point.

"But see? It's just a small place compared with Mexico. I think it's interesting to compare, because we haven't preserved too much in the United States. But San Miguel, back then at least, was a primitive place. It was like it was 200 years ago. There were many things we think of now as very quaint, but they weren't as convenient as modern living."

Is there a way to sum this up?

"I started to tell you that I feel like I've certainly had an adventurous and successful life as far as happy circumstances and the people I've met and a way of life that was entirely different from what I was used to. You become more adjusted to -- I wouldn't call it the slower pace because, good Lord, it takes you all day to do your errands when you can't park. But what makes you like a place? I love the look of Mexico, I love the Mexican people. I think they're wonderful people in the way they treat their families and the way they live. "Here you remember the good things and the old things."

Going back through fifty years of San Miguel, Betty Kempe has a lot of them to remember.

CHAPTER 8

WHERE'S OUR STUFF?

It's the sixth of August and they're newcomers, absolute beginners. They've been in San Miguel eighteen days. All they know is that the decision to do this was made eight months ago and now they're here. In transit by ship from Hawaii are their belongings. They don't expect to see them for a month, perhaps two. The container will land in Long Beach and come overland into Mexico. Everything they do is tentative, uncertain.

I decided to do a two-part conversation with a newly arrived couple to get a snapshot of the chaos that accompanies a relocation like this. In five months I'll come back and talk with them again to compare the reality with the anticipation. I have a sense myself of how much things can change in that amount of time. After the initial shock the changes are incremental, often nearly invisible. When you wake up one day and realize that in your mind you're in a different place from when you arrived, it's not clear how you got there.

Meanwhile Kip and Marjann are camped out in their house on Loreto just across and down a bit from the electric company. It'll be handy when it comes time to pay the bill every other month. Loreto is an old street in the oldest part of town. Some of their house is eighteenth century, other parts are two years old. With some effort and expertise and a fair amount of money, it could be a real charmer. It has good bones, but right now, some of it needs help. Marjann had been looking forward to this; she has a strong interest in interior design.

The one story facade is nondescript—it's part of the eighteenth century portion—and like most facades here, it suggests nothing about the interior. Just inside the entry are stacked bags of cement. To the right, directly behind the street wall is the *sala*, the living room, where the corner gas fireplace has been demolished, leaving an irregular scar on the wall. It was identical to several throughout the rest of the house, Kip says, a brick construction thickly painted over. It might have been from an apartment building in Cleveland. They couldn't wait to get rid of it.

Last week during a rainstorm Kip and Marjann accumulated a five-foot diameter puddle in the middle of the sala floor. As we talk today a crew of three is working on the roof, resealing skylights. I greet them warmly; they are the same men who painted my house and refinished the floors.

Yet the impression of the house is strong. The surfaces are a blend of white stucco, old stone, inlaid tiles, and architectural details like arches and decorative stone windows. The property has four separate structures, and as you wander through from the entry, small garden opportunities present themselves. There are also garden spaces atop both the first and second floors that furnish rooftop views toward the churches of *centro*. To the north the vista is more extended, encompassing the city as it climbs the hills above the highway to Dolores Hidalgo.

For this conversation we are seated in a small patio between the kitchen and a bedroom. The roof above is furnished by the second floor roof garden. An oriental rug anchors the table we sit at, partly covering the Saltillo tile floor.

"We found out about San Miguel from some friends of ours," says Kip. "They're from the Big Island of Hawaii and they said, 'You have to come and see this town.'" Everyone understood at first that a visit was all they meant, even though the friends had a home here. Kip and Marjann had no thought of leaving Honolulu, and they'd had a vacation home in Spain since 1992.

"When we came we rented a place for a month two years ago, and it was May, the hottest month. The place had a picture window exposed to the afternoon sun. It was so hot we practically had to spray water on ourselves. So I thought it was going to be hot a lot of the time, but when we came back now, in July, it was cool."

"Well, that [first trip] was just a discovery trip," adds Marjann, "primarily to discover if we could find a piece of property here, it being closer in distance to our home in Hawaii than going to our holiday home in Spain. It's halfway around the world from Hawaii. We thought if we could do that we'd buy a little place in Mexico. The places we saw here, that we could do an exchange for around $300,000 American, were not anything we wanted. We insist on being within walking distance of everything. Right now we don't have a car, and we don't care about it at this point." They decided there was no reason to sell the place in Spain. Nothing happened on that first trip other than looking at nearly fifty places for sale. Two years later they returned for another holiday, this time in October of 2007. "We had no intention of buying anything, or retiring, or of ever leaving Hawaii," says Marjann.

Once here, the agent who rented them their vacation house suggested they stop and look at a house for sale that was right on their way home from his office. They gave him a lukewarm yes. "We stood across the street," she continues, "because as sometimes happens they didn't have the proper key and had to run back to the office. We stood over there and just chatted, with no anticipation of walking in here. I wasn't even paying attention to the outside of the place; I wasn't put off by the way it looked, because it looked not too great. We didn't even chat about what this might be.

"But the moment that Kip and I walked in this door, I said, 'I feel like I'm in a palace.' Visually it wasn't exactly a palace, but it gave me that feeling. It immediately had a kind of warmth or spirituality, and I looked at Kip and he smiled at me, and I don't know who said it first, but I think you did. [Looking at Kip] I think you said, 'Would you give up Hawaii to be here?' We hadn't even passed the courtyard. We were five steps inside the door, and I said 'yes.'"

There had been no prior discussion, but they both realized the only way to buy the Loreto house was to sell the penthouse condo with ocean views in Honolulu. This also meant retirement and leaving the friends they'd had in Hawaii for more than thirty years. It meant leaving the United States. This looks to me much like the falling off the cliff experience, where in three seconds, with no discussion, they have both decided to upend their lives.

"That *was* a moment, wasn't it!" says Kip. He is a little breathless remembering it.

"That was a moment. It meant retiring, which had always been on my mind, but I was never ready to make a decision that it's time to quit, because I liked the money. When you're in a condominium you can buy something grander, but then something goes out while something new comes in." She pauses for a moment, as if focused on what they didn't choose to bring with them. "But it was an opportunity to retire from being a free lance court reporter for twenty-nine years."

"Which she hated from moment one," interjects Kip.

"I never really enjoyed it because I'm a more creative person in mind and heart than that ever allowed me to be. If you get creative as a court reporter you'll lose your job."

"For me," says Kip, "I liked the idea of having a little more space. Every time I walked through [the condo] I had to think about not bumping into something. It was time."

"Thirty-seven years," Marjann says from across the cast iron table, looking him in the eye.

"When we walked through this town we loved the *age* of it," he adds. "It made us feel that we were in Spain. We fell in love with Spain seventeen years ago, and the distance has just gotten too far; it takes us a week to recover from the flight. The American dollar, the value is not there now. [Here] we were able to get what we'd always wanted."

"I have always wanted to be a minority in another country," says Kip. "We were a minority in Hawaii."

"It's only 25% Caucasian," she adds.

But Kip had an air conditioning business to wrap up, so they arranged for the seller of their new old house to live in it while they returned to Honolulu. Almost a year later, they're back, and the dream and the reality have intersected—always a difficult time.

I ask what they expect to spend to bring this house up to their standard.

Kip gives Marjann a searching glance. It seems like they haven't spelled this out before. "It depends," he says. "If we have to change out this whole kitchen, that would be another fifteen or twenty easy," an unremarkable amount, but that's in Mexico. I've seen kitchen remodels in the States where that much got you the refrigerator and the towel bars, maybe part of the floor.

"I've never thought about an amount," she responds. "I'm not really concerned about it."

"My buddy said right off the bat, 'Ha! you've got fifty.' I'm hoping thirty. Right now we just want the roof to stop leaking. The skylights weren't put in properly."

"Is this a honeymoon period for you two?" I ask. "Are you in a glow from just being here?"

Marjann jumps on this one before Kip can open his mouth. "Absolutely not!" she says, leaning across the table at me.

"We're busy every day," he says, "trying to find people to do the things that we need to do. The main thing I wanted to get done was to seal the house. We had a little lake in the living room during that big storm last week." When Kip and Marjann had allowed their seller to stay on, rent free, it was on the condition that he repair a number of problems he was aware of when he put the house on the market. They left money with him to pay for materials and subcontractors. "We let him stay here so he could fix some stuff, which he didn't do," says Kip.

The conversation rambles on about the deficiencies of this arrangement, but their position is, what else could we do? There was no way they could wind down their lives in Hawaii in less than eight months. Kip was part owner of a business, and he couldn't just give notice in that situation. The new house could not be managed from 2,000 miles out in the Pacific. My own sense is that the inefficiencies and losses involved in moving to another country are often substantial and usually unpredictable. The moving costs are high and sometimes not everything arrives. The things that go missing can be senseless, not what you would imagine.

The eight-month process of dismantling their lives in Hawaii presented more challenges than they'd anticipated. Marjann's Korean hairdresser suggested that bad things would happen to make it easier for them to leave, an old proverb. "After two months of walking around gingerly in San Miguel," Marjann relates, speaking of cobblestone pavements and gaping holes in the terrain, "watching exactly where I was walking, I was home five days on the flat and I was running in a rain storm and fell and broke the ball off my humerus and broke my jaw." Her jaw was wired shut for two months, and she was in therapy for six.

"Then in May, before we left in July, our dog of nine years died. That was very, very hard to lose her. Leaving all my friends for the last thirty years, leaving my career, which was my identity. As much as I didn't enjoy it, it gave me a chance to dress up and be with interesting people, the movers and shakers of Honolulu. Then saying goodbye to these antique possessions that I'd been so pleased to bring into our lives. "So saying goodbye to the friends, my dog, my house, my career, I'm still in a state of sadness. I'm not really happy to be here yet."

I ask how long she thinks, or hopes, it might take to move on from that and settle in to San Miguel. "It won't happen until our belongings get here. Isn't that horrible?"

Does Kip have the same sense of loss?

"No. Men open one door and close another," he says immediately.

"Women grieve and men replace," I suggest.

When Kip goes on to say he didn't have that many close friends, Marjann thinks that's typical of men. He feels his church will seriously miss him, since he directed the music and managed the grounds and buildings.

I wonder if this feels to them like they're out of control. While Kip claims to feel a little more in control than he did a week ago, Marjann says in a sad tone, "I'm not feeling in control at all."

I ask what would make her feel in control at this point. "I think I don't want to get in control now. I'd like to wait for my things to get here. I think I might, like you said, grieve for a while. I don't have my exercise mat to lay on a clean floor and do my routine. I don't have my dog, which is like my teddy bear. I'm sleeping on sheets that are not as high count as I'd like. I want my nest, and I can't see it happening until my stuff is here." But in six months, she *knows* she will be feeling much better.

"I think we'll be less self-centered," adds Kip, "because right now it's all about what we've got to do for us. We're not reaching out too much."

Speaking about the general condition of the house when they took possession on their return, "We were a little naive," says Kip. "We didn't know that the roof and walls would be as porous as they are." I'm seeing porous as a euphemism here.

"I'm not so concerned about that," Marjann says. "The [important] fact is that the old walls are still standing from the 1700s; I don't care whether they leak. I just want them to stay standing. I love the feel of it. I love the energy of the place. The walls are not going to go down in our lifetime. Kip likes to come in and fix up places, so I knew it would be no problem."

If there is an unstated agenda, however, it's that the leaks ought to be plugged by the time their furnishings arrive.

In the meantime Marjann is alive to any small comfort. "Kip knows how to make things happen. I said to him last night, 'My water won't stay in the bathtub and I've tried five different plugs and I can't make them work because the tile is uneven where the drain is, so none of them can grab it.' So he cut one of the covers for me last night so the edge didn't extend outward too far. We did a test, and the water was still in the tub this morning. "I was so looking forward to my first bath where I didn't have to keep my heel over the drain to keep the water from draining out. I even tried sitting on it backwards with my butt over the drain. I'm very happy this morning, from something as simple as that."

"That's how I feel when I can find the right light bulb or the right screw," says Kip. "Any little thing gives us hope."

When the chaos ends, what will they do? Sometimes my own suspicion is that it doesn't end, but I have to ask this question, and then in five or six months we'll see if they ever got to do any of it. "Build relationships," says Kip, without hesitation, "make new friends, explore the country. If I see a need where I could help make something better I usually participate in it."

"Kip is a helper," she adds, "that's been his job in life, I think."

In the end, why did they come here? They were settled in what for a lot of people is a dream vacation place. Marjann professed to loving it there. They had spoken about all the times they would say to each other, "How would we live anywhere else?" They could have chucked their jobs and just kicked back, kept the climate, kept their friends, their Honolulu penthouse with a beach and city lights view and simply *deleted* everything they didn't like from their lives. Instead they threw it all away for something exotic but much less certain, or was that the appeal?

"Everything was at hand, everything was easy," she says. "It was the fat life. Instant hot water at the faucet. It would have been an easy thing to do just to stay there. But we felt that as long as we were in good health and we can make a move, it would be better to do that than just kick back. It just wasn't going to be *exciting* enough."

"For me, from the visits we had here," says Kip, "I love the multi-generational interaction of the Mexican people. That for me just goes straight to my heart."

"We like going back in time," she says. "We can get what we loved about Spain right here, and at a better price." Yet in six months when she looks back at this, "I'm just going to be glad that it's over. I'm in a sad place. I can still cry thinking about my dog."

❀❀❀

Five months have passed. It's enough time to be either settled in or counting up your regrets and rethinking the whole idea. At this point you can hardly believe how much you didn't know when you arrived. Having watched the slow accumulation of changes, you suspect that this process continues indefinitely. Six months from today you'll look back and think how naive you were now. When we last talked, Kip and Marjann had just finished mopping up the pool in the living room. "We think we have it tight now," says Kip, "but we don't really know. We weren't having any more leaks in the living room, but we weren't having any more big rains either." The test is coming, but now all of their things have arrived and are artfully arranged throughout the house, especially on the flood plain of the living room. They have a lot of art, nothing modern, but many pictures of the last 200 years. Their furniture is eclectic and the floors host many small rugs, mostly Turkish prayer rugs. Each window treatment is unique and striking. If the effect is not precisely Mexico, neither is it Honolulu. Most likely it's Marjann.

Progress has been immense, and the largest project remaining is the garden. "In Spain," says Kip, "we tried to do it ourselves, and we wished we had gotten a little more help. We'd like to get things in before the rain starts."

Other than the flooding, few other problems have occurred. There were small issues of the absence of power to sconces and chandeliers, and one ceiling fixture fell during the night. They have never had the feeling they should have rented for a while before buying. It was the house that was their main reason for moving. Living in *centro* has not been a problem; the street is fairly quiet and the fireworks have not been excessive. I suggest they should wait for May, with the fiesta of Santa Cruz, before they make their final judgment on that.

When we talked in August they felt that when the chaos ended they would spend their time building relationships. "Well, I don't think it's quite ended yet. It's dwindled," says Kip.

"Fernando [one of the workers] was practically living here," adds Marjann. "It calmed down about two weeks before Christmas. There's still work going on. Just an hour ago we had the ironworker here. It hasn't stopped, but I can see there's light at the end of the tunnel now."

But the chaos has effectively shut down their social life. They've turned down several invitations. Now they suspect they won't be invited again. "They read into it all kinds of things when somebody says no," says Kip.

"We really haven't formed any relationships," says Marjann, almost in a tone of surprise, almost as if she's been too busy to think about it. "We're too tired at the end of the day."

Kip's original hope of staying within $30,000 on the renovations has not been far off the mark. He thinks they're still under $35,000, but the only thing they've done in the kitchen is some alteration of the tile work. They've opted to go with the existing cabinetry for now.

Part of their original decision to move to San Miguel was that it would be exciting. They gave up what Marjann called "the fat life" to come here. Has it been exciting? Kips feels it has, but adds that, "she hasn't started to feel really good until..."

"About a month ago," she breaks in. "About then I started to feel like it was becoming our home. I like my privacy. I don't like workers here all the time. I don't even really like having a maid here three days a week. But, exciting? I think it's going to be more exciting when I get involved in language lessons, or in things that I want to do rather than what has to be done. Now that my furniture has arrived and I've gotten things set up, I don't miss our place in Honolulu at all."

"Honolulu was very transient," says Kip. "You invest time and energy in people and suddenly they're gone."

Both feel there has not been a moment when they regretted their move. But what about the water and the humidity? "How about your skin?" I ask Marjann. "Oh! My skin has aged a couple of years in just six months, easily."

"We thought it would be more dusty," adds Kip. "We've got a house being built next to us, two doors down. It took out the *Parroquia* view from my bedroom."

I ask whether they felt they had prepared themselves well enough. "We've lived in Spain," says Kip, "so we knew what it was like to scramble around in a Spanish speaking place and try to find stuff."

"We took a good six months getting organized," adds Marjann. "I was down, thinking about everything. We had time. I don't think there's anything I would have done differently. Maybe a couple of pieces that I sold."

"I think we would have bought more sheets and towels if we had known how hard it is to get that stuff here." Kip is referring to the 600 count Egyptian cotton

Marjann favors.

After five and a half months they are still new-comers by most definitions, but what would they say to people just arriving? "You've got to be patient, and I would network to try to find the right help. I think we've been pretty lucky with people we've used."

"We didn't realize how expensive things were going to be at Liverpool [San Miguel's only department store]," adds Marjann. "Anything that comes from the U.S. is expensive. I paid $12 for a Pyrex four cup measuring cup."

"Bring your specialty light bulbs," says Kip. "And when you're buying a place, find out about the neighbors before you buy. We didn't check and we just got lucky."

They're clearly reaching for things to warn the next person about. Five and a half months into it, they've almost nothing to complain about.

CHAPTER 9

LIKE PICKING WEEDS OUT OF GRAVEL

S ometimes many years can pass between planting a seed and seeing it germinate. For Carl Selph, the number was thirty.

In 1960 he was teaching English at the University of North Carolina in Greensboro and took a semester off, thinking he would go to Japan. He had already bought a steamer ticket when he realized he probably couldn't afford four and a half months there. Europe, where he had visited a couple of years earlier, was equally out of his price range.

"A friend of mine knew people who had moved down here, and I had seen in *Holiday Magazine* a full page photo of San Miguel. I thought maybe I could afford Mexico. So I came down here on a bus in 1960. At that time there was no bus station, you got off in front of the Parroquia (the main church on the plaza). I stepped down with my suitcase and decided immediately I was in love with San Miguel."

During those five months he stayed mostly in San Miguel, but took a few side trips to Mexico City, Taxco, and Acapulco. "I liked it so much that the next year I came back for about two months."

We are sitting in a rental house on Fray Pedro de Gante, on a hill at the edge of the Independencia neighborhood, just off the Libramiento that goes out of town to Dolores Hidalgo. Across the street and down about fifty meters is a wide property fronted by a white wall. This lot runs through to the street beyond, where it abuts a green space that would like to be a park some day.

Beyond the white wall Carl Selph's new 7,000 square foot house is going up. U-shaped in plan, it embraces a deep garden with a fountain in the center. The structure is fully up and two stories high, but there are no finishes yet except several *boveda* ceilings, four-cornered decorative red brick vaults built by a man on a scaffold. He uses a bucket of mortar, a pile of bricks, a trowel and a length of string. It's not high-tech, but the result is stunning. There are the normal public rooms, four bedroom suites, an office, two second-floor terraces overlooking the gardens, and a roof garden with the required long views.

For a man who will live here alone, Carl is only minimally apologetic. Maybe, at age 77, this, his twenty-first building project, is his last, or maybe it's not. Everything is for sale, he says. If someone wants to buy it, then he'll build something else. Retirement is not on the horizon. He equates it with boredom, and boredom with death. He has little interest in either.

Carl is tall and still good-looking with a mostly full head of white hair. His voice retains the soft character of his rural Arkansas upbringing, although he has always been, he says, a professional exile, having lived more than half his life abroad.

During that first trip to San Miguel Carl tried to get a job teaching creative writing at the Insitiuto Allende.

"Stirling Dickinson, who was the head of if it, said he couldn't use me because I didn't have a work permit." He then tried at a college in Mexico City, with the same result. After his two month visit, the following year he went to Italy. In 1964 he returned to Mexico for another brief visit. Eventually, he taught at the University of Maryland, the Azores, Labrador, Newfoundland, Iceland. Following that he settled in Italy for nineteen years more.

"I decided then I should move back to the States, bought a big house in a beautiful little town in North Carolina, and realized almost immediately I'd made a big mistake. It was difficult to go from Florence to a town of 3,500 people, but it was beautiful. A friend of mine in that town owned a house down here, and she said, 'Why don't you take off for the month of August and go back down there.' So I came down and had a wonderful month and realized I should have looked around before I moved back to the States."

This was in 1987. It was the first time he'd spent any time in Mexico in twenty-three years and it told him what he had to do. Returning to North Carolina he began to try to figure out how to get rid of his beautiful 1910 house. Finally, in April of 1990, he returned to San Miguel and rented a small house on Aldama for four years. He did not speak Spanish, but Italian, which, he says, made Spanish more difficult. The closeness of many words was more confusing than helpful.

At that time, the downtown area, *centro*, looked much like it had earlier, just better painted. "There used to be grocery stores there, but they're all gone now. In those days [the 1960s] there were no one-way streets, and practically nobody had a telephone. If you got invited, there would be a knock at the door and a maid would be there with a note saying could you come to lunch at two o'clock and you'd say yes and send her back. "In 1960 the first good restaurant opened downtown, but a great deal of this development for tourism has happened since I've been living here, since 1990."

But Carl, once he'd returned to live here, did not know what he was going to do for a living. He still had to make payments on his North Carolina house, which, in a town full of other beautiful houses, was not selling. Finally it did sell, and he received a small inheritance at about the same time. He decided to build a house in San Miguel. "I found a lot out in the Mexiquitos neighborhood that had two little mirror image structures started, the foundations and a little bit of wall, and I figured out a way to link them and make an attractive little house."

He was able to complete the project without using a contractor. The second person who looked at the property bought it. For someone shopping for a livelihood there was a clear message in this. Eventually he took on a business partner and either built himself or, in participation with others, twenty houses.

"Right now I don't have anything for sale. I'm building this one to live in, but it will always have a price on it. I don't have much faith in architects." He's always designed his own houses. I wondered if it was because he'd had a bad experience with an architect.

"The only bad experience I've had was seeing what they do. The new houses that they design here are too complicated, especially because a lot of older people move here. They think that where there's no need for a step up or a step down, it makes the house more interesting to have them. They often don't have square corners. They think for some reason that rooms shaped like this (his arms indicate a floor plan of nightmarish angles) are more attractive. Of course, you can't place furniture in them. "When I design a house I try to design it with a good traffic pattern, for light, air, and an easy way to arrange furniture that works."

This sounded too much like common sense to me. And does he plan to keep doing it?

"Well, I'm 77 years old and a half. What I'm hoping is that this one I'm building will be my last major effort, although I may build some spec houses. The competition is pretty fierce right now, and the market's terrible."

Construction and design have been only a part of his activities in San Miguel. When he lived in *centro* there was the literary magazine. He had long been a poet, and self published his collected poems just last year. "We used to have Sunday literary readings, and I was very much involved with that. I had not been writing for a long time––I stopped when I was about thirty-five––and I was down here on a visit in about '87 or '88, before I moved back here. I started writing again and publishing again. That went on until about 2001, and then I figured that I'd finished the poetry. Last year I decided to publish the book mostly for friends and family."

He has also published three short stories over the years and written a novel that has never been published. He is clear that it never will be.

"We had a magazine here called *San Miguel Writer*. We published several issues over a period of a few years and I was one of the editors. Our problem was that it was all or almost all in English and our only market was here and there was no sponsorship for it."

Carl Selph has found it's possible to have friends among Mexicans. He finds them very family oriented, and when there's a gathering the families are included. It reminds him of his upbringing in south Arkansas.

"When we had a dinner, which would be midday, it was for family. My mother, it never crossed her mind to invite a good friend for lunch. That's the way everybody did it there. In Italy it was pretty much the same way. The Florentines like to say, 'We Florentines are closed,' and they're proud of it.

"Here I have found the people to be friendly, pleasant to deal with, hard working. But I have not been invited to many Mexican homes. It's like it was in Italy. I used to entertain a lot, and I never had any Italians say no to an invitation, but I didn't get invited back. With some of the friends this went on for years, with others I was very much invited to their homes."

He returns to the States once or twice a year, for both family visits and shopping.

Even after being away for eighteen years he prefers to monitor events in the States closely. "I read *The New York Times* on the web every morning. I find the television here so bad that I have great difficulty finding anything to look at."

I remark that the level of contact with events in the States is something that varies widely among people I talked to. "Well, you know," he went on, "I have been a foreigner anywhere I've lived, including the United States. This earth is not my home. But I am fascinated by what's going on in politics. I am a Yellow Dog Democrat. It means that if nobody were running for office except a yellow dog, I'd vote for the yellow dog rather than a Republican.

"I have found that living abroad is a kind of escapism because I can watch what goes on here in politics without any involvement because it isn't my country. I am still very American, but I'm American as of about 1960. By 1962, anyway, I was living mostly outside the United States. When I go up there I don't know how to do certain things, I don't know how much stamps cost, I don't know how to operate those little machines for credit cards."

There are ways in which Mexico reminds him of Italy. "San Miguel is a Mexican version of a Tuscan hill town. But I had more in common with a lot of Italians than with a lot of Mexicans. For example, there's a place in Florence, right downtown, where they sell lottery tickets, and I used to see a big crowd, like 50 men, standing around talking, all the time. One day I asked a friend of mine, 'What are they talking about?'

"And he said they were talking about abstract art. Now, that's the Florentines. There's a certain provinciality about the Florentines, because they are very sure that they are the best looking, the smartest, and the most talented people on earth. And I think they probably are. They just don't realize that they stopped doing anything after the Renaissance.

"Here you're dealing with a very different kind of society, where there are those who are very high up and well off and powerful, and those who are at the bottom."

How does the contrast of that great wealth and the great poverty effect him personally?

"This may sound snobby, but I had lived down here for years and I always had a maid who did the laundry. When I got back to the States I realized I couldn't afford one, and also, to my horror, I found I had to pump my own gas. I decided I wanted to go to a country that pumped my gas for me and where I could afford a maid. The woman who's working for me now I've had for years and years, and I'll have her till I die, I suppose. She's in my will. She needs the job. She has almost no education, but she does what she does here very well. She takes care of me and I do what I can to take care of her."

This sounds to me like the "more bang for the buck" argument, a dollar simply goes further in Mexico than at home. Carl agrees. "I have never had much money, sometimes it's been hand to mouth. I had a maid in Italy who said to me once, 'You could probably do everything I do as well as I can or better.' I said, 'Yes I can.' I grew up with no sisters, two brothers, younger, and so we all learned to do everything. I milked the cow every day, I fed the chickens, I helped my father cut down trees for wood for the fire. I don't feel that when I hire somebody to do what they can do best that I'm taking advantage of them because I've done jobs dirtier than that."

Does living in San Miguel involve sacrifices as well as the benefits of the dollar going further? "Yes," he says, "but it's my own fault. I liked Florence, and I liked New York even though I didn't necessarily take advantage of all the cultural offerings; they were always reassuringly there. Here there's a lot going on, and a lot of it, especially the music, is world class. I do get to concerts once in a while. But I would, [in Florence] like on Sunday mornings, go to the Uffizi [Gallery].

"This is a famous place, and many people want to live here, but at the same time it's really a hick town in the country with an overlay of mostly gringo culture. I love the look of the place, the weather, the way I can live here that I could not afford to in the States. I don't plan to move and I'm very grateful that Mexico lets me live here."

So is Carl Selph an exile? An expatriate? What term could cover all of this?

"I would say that I find living outside the United States less provoking and more interesting than living in the United States. If I could live long enough, I would live everywhere there is in this world. I heard long ago, don't do anything longer than ten years. I've not obeyed that, but I think that's the way I'd like to live my life."

He's not certain he's much different from many Americans who moved here about the time he did, 1990. But he is different from most Americans who are moving here now.

"When I was first down here people were not building houses with marble floors. People came down here (in the 60s) because they had artistic interests, whether they were very good painters or writers or not. They could live here because the climate was great, the people were great, and the town was cheap. The enormous house across from the Peralta [Theater] that is now a bed and breakfast and a restaurant, belonged to people I knew. Those people bought that house. It was one of the old *mesones* and had a back yard which was where the mule trains full of silver used to be placed overnight. It was so big that in the back yard they built a two story three bedroom house. They bought all of that property for $8,000.

"In those days you could come down here with not much and live well and pleasantly. It was a much simpler town, no traffic problems, you could park anywhere, very few cars, very few telephones. The people who had telephones would let friends use them. I was totally charmed by it."

Now, with increased traffic and tourism, [the reason he left Florence], he feels San Miguel is in danger of becoming a Disney version of a Mexican town.

Reinvention of himself has been a basic feature of Carl Selph's entire life. He went from college in Arkansas to graduate school at Columbia, simply because it was in New York. It was the only school he applied to. He moved to teach in North Carolina in the same department as Randall Jarrell, who was a successful and widely respected poet but had recurring mental problems. "He simply walked out of the hospital and his wife says it was an accident, but I think he stepped in front of a car on purpose."

Selph remained in teaching for about 10 years and finally got tired of grading freshman theme papers. He knew he did not want a Ph.D., did not want to be a professional scholar. "I had been to Florence and a friend said there's a language school for sale and would you like to be a partner in it. So we bought it. There was nothing much but a few desks and a blackboard. We ran that until the big flood in 1966, which pretty much annihilated business. In 1969, with another American partner, I started an export business. I was selling everything from baby furniture to tomb stones," he recalls. "Decorators and architects were my biggest clients. I did that for seventeen years and then I sold out to him and moved to the States."

When Selph returned to San Miguel he began drawing plans again as he began building houses. "It was an enormous satisfaction to put something down on paper and then actually walk through the rooms."

Now there is nothing that would make him move back to the States. He plans to be cremated here when he dies and have his remains buried in the family plot in Arkansas. For the rest of his family there is a lack of comprehension about why he stays. "They enjoy coming down here, but they would never dream of leaving Arkansas. That's the only place they'd ever live."

They miss what Carl sees here every day, and maybe it's something not everyone can see.

"Sometimes, I must say, over the years, I've been on a roof terrace or a patio downtown having lunch with a beautiful temperature, beautiful skies, and I think there's no place on earth I'd rather be than right here. I have that experience a lot of times."

I wondered if it happened for him more in San Miguel than in Italy.

"In Italy, for the last eleven years that I was there, I rented a big ancient farmhouse thirty-five minutes from my apartment in Florence. That was, and maybe still is, my favorite spot on earth. I used to go out there not so much in the winter, because Florence has cold winters, and that house had nothing but a couple of fire places. I used to go out there the middle weekend in March and clean house to get ready for summer. I was out there once sitting on the gravel of the terrace, pulling up weeds. A friend of mine was on a ladder clipping back the limbs of an acacia tree, and it was probably about four in the afternoon. I thought, I have never been so happy in my life, sitting there in the gravel, pulling weeds.

"It's comparable to moments I've had here, when nothing particularly exciting was going on, but I was perfectly happy and didn't want to be anywhere else. I think this is a town that affords those moments pretty often if you sit quietly and wait for them. I am very glad that at the age of 77 and a half I am able to live in this beautiful town in a country that is hospitable to me and live in a pleasant way with the generous help of Graciela, who works for me, and still to be doing things. I still want to build houses, I still would like to write some more, I would like to travel some more. I went to Turkey in October. Turkey was the last place I hadn't been that I really wanted to go to."

Retirement is not a word he can easily locate in his vocabulary. "One of the problems I've had is easy boredom, and so I think if I had no projects in mind I'd probably die right away." You could argue that Carl Selph is rather driven for his age. Not many people in their upper seventies want to be that busy. I can't disagree with that, but at the same time I find a remarkable serenity in his attitude that seems to coexist quite well with all the things he's involved in.

It's as if part of him is always back at the farmhouse outside Florence pulling weeds from the gravel.

It's not a bad place to be at any age.

CHAPTER 10

WE THOUGHT WE HAD RETIRED

You might say that Mary and Gil Rapp settled here because they were blown seriously off course.

"We thought we had retired to Fairhope, Alabama," says Mary, "but we weren't as happy about that as we thought we would be. We went through a hurricane there [in 1989], which did a lot of destruction. Gil just pronounced that he never wanted to own another house, which economically was a dumb decision, because the difference between prices then and prices now is just incredible. Here we've rented several places."

But they couldn't get out immediately; it took nearly a year to repair and sell the Alabama house.

The Rapps had known about San Miguel since the 60s, when they had visited Mexico with their children. Among the many places they had stopped, this small city stood out for its charm. "The fact that it was an art center was a huge attraction to us," says Mary, who has been a painter all her life. "The Instituto at that time was really a going operation, and it was very attractive. We walked in and Mozart was playing in the sculpture studio. The view, from the back, of the *Parroquia*, it was just idyllic."

Since the late 40s the Insitituto had been a magnet for GIs wanting to study art under the GI Bill after World War II. Some saw no reason to leave, and this migration launched the American colony here. Mary Rapp was impressed by the fact that David Siqueiros, one of the big three Mexican muralists (with Diego Rivera and Jose Orozco), had worked here in the 40s, painting murals in the old chapel of the Bellas Artes, another art school, one established in a former convent. She had studied at Washington University in St. Louis with Max Beckmann, the great German Expressionist the Nazis had forced out before the War.

"We came back down here in 1989 [after the Alabama hurricane]," continues Mary, "to decide how we felt about it, and we actually moved here in 1990. I had quite a few artist friends, and writers who had been here right after the war. We knew a lot about San Miguel before we got here." Their children, a son in Houston and a daughter in Spokane, had been married and on their own for a long time at this point.

During his working life Gil sold contract floor covering to institutions. "I once did a prison. It was a kind of remodeling at the site where Geronimo had been imprisoned, a place called Mount Vernon, Alabama. It was an old army prison. It was then converted into a mental institution, and the general contractor was having a great deal of trouble because the Indians had tunneled out. They didn't escape, they just came and went."

The Rapps spoke no Spanish at all initially, but quickly enrolled in classes. The home they rent now is part of a former manager's quarters in the Fabrica la Aurora, the same art studio, gallery, and antiques venue where Linda Vandiver rents her art space. Gil lost his sight eight years ago and they needed a home near Mary's studio so she could be available if there was a problem. She's not much more than 100 feet away.

Despite being part of a former textile factory, the apartment has a great deal of charm, with high ceilings and a large living room with an ornate and elegant fireplace. There are two garden areas and the light is beautiful. Sitting in their dining area looking out toward the long garden space, I can see that the only reason to have her studio in the main part of the factory is for the visitor traffic.

In her 80s now, Mary is trim and vigorous. Her grooming is elegant, and speaking with her I have the sense of encountering a penetrating intelligence.

"When we returned in 1990 we immediately met a lot of people we felt very much at home with, in every sense. At that time I would say the general population of the expatriates was a little more intellectual than they are now. It was an interesting and mixed group of people."

I suggest that others had mentioned this as well. I'm thinking of Betty Kempe, who'd first been here in the late 50s.

"It's an entirely different group, mostly," Mary continues. "Some of them were extremely nice and a lot of very interesting people still come, but I feel now that a large number of people are coming for second homes and are not as committed to full time living here. The homes they're building are appalling to me, they're so huge. I find that's a little bit disturbing. I wonder what the future is in that sense."

We speak for a while about people who came at about the same time as the Rapps. Carl Selph was in that group, and the Rapps socialized with him. Another was the actress Olivia Cole, who was in *Roots*.

"There was a very interesting group," adds Gil, "of retired middle class Jewish people who supported almost every artistic activity, including the chamber music series."

"We both love chamber music," says Mary, "in fact I ended up on the board of that for several years. That was one of the attractions, the music, the art scene, the people, the weather. After the soggy Alabama experience, that was pretty wonderful."

I mention that Betty Kempe had suggested that the Instituto had come down a bit from its lofty past.

"It's been ruined," says Mary, "it's been destroyed. The people who inherited it didn't have much foresight about where it was going. At one point the Chicago Institute was interested in purchasing it as an offshoot of their organization. The owners, little by little, lost most of the good teaching staff. Now it's primarily the site for craft fairs."

The Instituto is a vast property on San Antonio. It dates from the early to mid eighteenth century and now houses a number of restaurants and galleries, but teaching activity in painting and sculpture is greatly reduced. Talk of the ups and downs of this place and some of the great characters who worked there and at the Bellas Artes brings up the story of Masha Beyo. "Did anyone talk to you about the *pastorelas*?" asks Mary. "They were done by this marvelous woman. Was she Hungarian, Gil?"

"No, I believe she was Danish."

"The amusing part of this was that her name was spelled Beyo, and she did the *pastorelas* every year, which were the Spanish fables of the birth of Christ. It was in the Bellas Artes. They had people strung on wires. It was fantastic. She was an actress and ballet dancer married to a Hollywood actor. She was a fabulously powerful person and beloved by the Mexicans for putting on this wonderful thing and training so many of them in dance and theater. When she died, they had a mass for her and they dedicated a room to her, and instead of spelling her name Beyo, it's Bello."

It's sounding to me that many of the old marvelous locals are gone. Is the town itself getting better, or is it fading away and turning into something else?

"It's changing, and I would say that in some ways it's gone up. When we first got here it was difficult to get a telephone. Many products were totally unavailable. We made trips back to the States to buy things. Now you can go to Querétaro and get anything you want, and you almost don't have to go to Querétaro, because it's coming here with Soriana [a supermarket] and places like that. But the character of the town has changed as a result. It's changed architecturally, with those huge monster buildings out on the edges."

"And the traffic is horrible," adds Gil.

How about making friends among the Mexicans, I ask, a thread that runs though most of these conversations.

"It's been rare," says Mary. "I have a few. I think it's a cultural issue. I've asked myself that, and I have not found them antagonistic in any sense. I have many friends who are Mexican, but they're not my close friends. I don't know if it's totally the upbringing. Religion is often an issue; they're mostly Catholic, but not all, by any means. I am sorry about that. I've been disappointed not to have more Mexican friends."

"The strong Mexican social group is impenetrable by most Americans," says Gil.

"I think there are some people who have made better inroads than I have," says Mary. "And the people I meet as a fellow artist, that's fine, but we have art in common and that helps bridge the gap."

Being in the Fabrica community, which is at once a support group, gallery space, studio, ongoing art walk, and social club is unique in itself. But living there as well must make it unlike any other community in San Miguel.

"It's a mixed group," says Mary, not one to sentimentalize things. "I would say we have a core group of artists—I was the second artist here—then it was pretty much still a factory with all the machines in place. Then a lot of people moved in and they were a mixed bag. Some of them were dedicated artists and some of them were very commercial. Then there were decorators. Now there's a shop selling handbags. It's becoming more of a mercantile, retail market. We're having a little tug of war now about whether it's all right for people to open when they feel like it or should there be a law that you have to stay open from eleven to six."

To me the Fabrica does not feel like an American development. It has the sense of having evolved within its own skin, a skin that is largely unaltered, leaving large chunks of it unchanged. Mary confirms this impression. "The Garay family owns it. This is a family from Spain. They own not only the Fabrica, but a lot of the land that surrounds it. It closed about fifteen years ago. I've heard various explanations why. I think a lot of it was competition from Asia. What they made was *manta*, which was that white muslin-looking fabric that you see the Mexicans wearing in all the old photographs and paintings. It's a cotton product; they had their own plantations north of here. The studio I'm in was the carding room were they took the seeds out of the cotton."

While Mary feels that being an artist in San Miguel is wonderful, it may not be in itself a living. This is not unique to San Miguel. "Well, if I were totally dependent on what I'm selling I'd be working harder at it and I wouldn't be living as well. But I *have* sold quite well, and people who like me really like me. Usually they're gringos from New York, California, Atlanta. People who are more sophisticated collectors."

She has had other gallery representation in the past but found that the packing and cross-border shipping of pictures was too problematical. "Also," she points out bluntly, "I'm old now."

I raise the issue of whether being in Mexico is more about what it has been or what it hasn't, expecting that the answer would fall squarely on what it was.

"It was a combination," says Mary. "Actually we had gotten to a point in Alabama where we felt that our lives had come to a dead end in many ways. I was teaching, but not in a stimulating atmosphere. I was teaching sculpture at that point, and I had gotten a lot of responsibilities for forming an art association there but it was like pulling teeth. Fairhope was a wonderful place. We had lived there in the 50s. It just wasn't the same. It was very disappointing, and we both felt stodgy and we weren't particularly happy with the politics. We're both political junkies and very much liberal Democrats."

"The first time we lived there," says Gil, "the town was 90% Democratic, and when we moved back the civil rights issue had really come up. The town had switched from 90% Democratic to 92% Republican."

"The opposite was true here," adds Mary, "everyone we met agreed with us politically. We got here just as the first Gulf War started." But they found a frustrating lack of news in English, and it was too difficult to follow when the Berlin Wall came down. It served to spark their efforts to improve their Spanish. Now they find it easier through cable TV and the Internet to stay in close touch with events in the U.S. There is also an English language newspaper from Mexico City called The News which they read regularly. "We still care a lot politically about the United States," says Mary, "and we're not anti-American in any sense."

Mary still goes back periodically, twice this year, but more normally once a year. She gets to New York when she can to keep track of what's happening in the art world. "I'm still very active as an artist and am about to be in the book on the San Miguel artists." She is also going to be interviewed by a scholar from St. Louis on the time she spent studying with Max Beckmann.

"This has been such a wonderful time to be here—not to sound elitist—but I can have somebody working for me so I don't have to do housework. I can do artwork, which is wonderful as I'm getting older, to say the least."

The ability to live better on fewer dollars has been a real plus for the Rapps. "That was a factor," says Mary "We had made some bad investments in the United States. We were OK, but we weren't having as much fun as we wanted."

Only a major political upheaval in Mexico would make them consider returning to the U.S. "Although," Mary says, "I get a certain amount of pressure from the children. 'What are we going to do—you remember how old you are—if you get sick.' But I would rather be here, I think, even ill, than I would be there, in many ways. Not necessarily for the quality of the medical care, but for the quality of the nursing care. The people here are so gentle. The hospitals are very well staffed and Querétaro [one hour away] is a major medical center. In fact, I had one hysterical experience. The first apartment we moved into, I went into the kitchen and there was a jar of white powder in the pantry, and I said, oh, I think that's salt. I took one taste of it and my throat started closing. We rushed to the clinic; I took the stuff with me. I waited and kept feeling worse. When we finally got in to a doctor I explained in my bad Spanish that I had done this and handed him the jar.

"He looked at it, reached over to the trash can, opened the lid, and dropped it in. He said, 'Don't take any more of that.' I'll never know what it was, but I think it was monosodium glutamate, which I am allergic to." Mary agrees with what others have said, that for a major procedure she would probably go back to the States, but mainly because she has Medicare.

"I went blind, eight years ago," says Gil, "and spent a great deal of time in the United States, had 11 operations and they did me absolutely no good. It was a type of glaucoma."

Other than the obvious involvement with cultural activities, the Rapps have done volunteer work as well.

"When we first got here, the Feed the Hungry program was very primitive, and we had a van, an old beat up van at that point. They didn't have the kitchen yet at all. What we did was go around to restaurants and get their left over food and take it out to the station, which was out in Los Rodriguez. There were no paved roads at all, so we'd get mired down in mud sometimes."

"We did that two or three years," says Gil.

"Then we both got very involved with the church, St. Paul's [Episcopal]. Gil was senior warden and then I was senior warden. We were talked into that. It was just at the time that the priest decided to leave."

"We also organized a film series," says Gil, "every Saturday. I had made a collection of films, French, Japanese, Chinese."

"It was Sunday," says Mary. "People would just come by. Sometimes we had the whole house packed and two TVs going with the tapes running. It was fun."

Things are quieter now. Since Gil lost his sight it's impossible for him to walk about because the sidewalks and streets are so irregular. They don't feel they have missed much beyond their grand kids and some friends. But do they have any regrets?

"Sure," Mary laughs, "money. I would have bought a house. That's an issue that's been between us. Other than that, I have no regrets. I feel that this has been a really creative period of my life. I do treasure the quality of life here, but I miss not being politically involved in anything that happens here. I feel constrained to stay completely out of it, and that is a little bit inhibiting because I'm normally a more participatory person. That has been a slight frustration."

"When I had my vision I really loved it. I like the Mexican people. They can be happy with so little material things that Americans would feel left out if they didn't have. Unfortunately the big stores coming in have changed the culture considerably. When I got out and was able to talk to a number of Mexican people they actually talked politics to me. But it's very hard to get political information from the natives."

"Well, there's Arturo, of course," says Mary. "He worked for us as a chauffeur for a while when Gil was losing his sight but was still getting out. Now he's back working for us part time. He had gone twice illegally to the United States, and he's talked to us a lot about that experience. But now he's afraid to go back. Because of the tightening up of things he might end up in jail. So communication has not been impossible. It's not a lack of communication, it's just the lack of a cultural—something—that prevents the really close bonding, I think."

Gil admits to being disappointed that he never was able to get more involved with the Mexican culture. He had expected that he would.

"I'm not sure I did," says Mary.

"You know we tried the first two or three years when we were active in St. Paul's."

"The outreach program," says Mary. "and trying to involve them in the church. We did make an effort to do that."

"And it failed totally."

Mary is no less frank on the American tourists she sees in San Miguel. "I wish they'd dress better; they're really gross. They've gotten so fat and they're all wearing shorts. But I've found that the people that come into my gallery are very nice, and by and large, ask interesting questions. I don't know whether that's because they're in an art gallery rather than in a shop. I feel that in the United States too."

Is there anything they would add that sums things up?

"One thing I haven't said that we felt very strongly when we first started coming down here, certainly in the 60s, and then even as late as the 90s, is that it was an experience that was like stepping back in time. In contrast to the United States there was a quality of feeling among people because they still lived in the community and outdoors. This had disappeared from the United States with television and air conditioning. People had become isolated in little family groups, and you never saw life in the street. To go back to seeing it again was very stimulating. I don't know how much it had to do with the work I started doing, but I think to some degree it did.

"Also the antiquities here, that we've visited quite a bit, really influenced me artistically. I was so impressed." By this Mary means the ancient cities.

Gil was born in a small town in southwestern Arkansas in the 20s, a place and time that now seems remote. "Life here, when we first came, reminded me a great deal of that. It was a 30-year retreat back in time, which was, in a way, charming. I remember when we drove down the first time people were covering themselves with banana leaves to protect themselves from the rain."

CHAPTER 11

RUINED FOR LIFE

Anna B. is a tall, imposing woman with an attractive face and lively eyes that suggest even before she speaks that she will not be holding much back. Her old one story house on Calle Jesus has a narrow facade without windows. How old it might be is difficult to guess, but the street has the feel of being undisturbed and inward looking. In New Orleans the house would be called a "shotgun," because the six rooms are lined up in single file, one leading into another, without an inner corridor. Outside, a long open air passage brings light to all the rooms and leads to a stairway at the back, access to her roof garden. Once up there, you wander over different levels until back near the street there is a small, framed view of the *Parroquia*.

Anna was born in Newcastle on Tyne, England just before World War II, and emigrated with her family to Toronto in 1950. There are many Canadians in San Miguel, and I'm hoping that her story will illuminate the American experience by contrast, for whatever she might be, she is emphatically not an American.

"I'm a very judgmental person," says Anna. "Coming from Canada, where we've been shoved around by Big Brother to the south and our politics have been interfered with, and nearly all of our companies are now subsidiaries of bigger American companies, you know, I already have a chip on my shoulder. I find that I feel a little bit on the outside of the foreign community life [here], because of not knowing where all the states are or what they do or who's the latest star or who's this hip singer. I often notice that when Canadians are around, they say where they're from and they always say Canada afterwards because if they don't, somebody will say, 'Huh?' where's that?'

"I'm just a little awkward about the fact that people can travel from one place to another and expect everything they had at home to be given to them. Americans are a little bit loud, and very lacking in courtesy. I was sitting painting on the street one day, in the middle of a water color, which you really don't stop in the middle of because you've got a wash to control, and someone came along and said, 'Do you live here?' (very loudly) 'How much money do you make and did you buy your house or do you rent?' Even at St. Paul's [Episcopal] Church, we were always praying for the president of the U.S. What about the queen?"

By her own account she settled in San Miguel because a three-year sojourn in Cuernavaca in the 60s had ruined her for life, for life anywhere other than Mexico. She didn't say it ruined her life, it was just that it took her a while to get back to Mexico, and it seemed too much like biding her time in between.

Anna B. first came to Mexico late in 1959 after being hired by the World Association of Girl Guides and Girl Scouts in Cuernavaca. "Here I came as a young innocent 23-year-old and found myself in this paradise of Mexico. I just fell in love with living in general." She had never been to Mexico before. The Girl Guides would come in from all over the world for six-day sessions. "I met several thousand girls in the course of working there. We gave them a program of arts and crafts and tours, campfires and fellowship, which really gave them a lot of understanding of each other and helped them to love Mexico."

In the following year her parents drove down from Toronto in November for a visit. Anna went up to Monterrey to help guide them down, and they spent a night in San Miguel on the way.

"It was a dirt road in, off Highway 57, and we spent the night in a hotel right on the square and really didn't think a great deal about it."

After three years working in Cuernavaca she returned to Toronto. "I never settled after that. I'd found Paradise too young. I worked in the University of Toronto Library, and I couldn't believe how menial my life had become. Whether I put a dot or a comma on a book spine was of major importance. I had been living in Mexico in this fabulous valley, looking at volcanoes, with the most incredible natural sights, wonderful ruins, and I never settled back again. I was ruined from then on."

Getting back proved to be less difficult than she thought, although it took a while. By that time she was teaching art and took a year's leave of absence. "I really must have been burnt out because I took three years. I was here [in San Miguel], living with my mom at that time. She was widowed by then. I had no income. I just lived very, very simply. Things were not so expensive then. It was the early 80s."

Anna's parents had earlier explored a number of places in Mexico, as far south as Oaxaca, and on the way back to Canada stopped again in San Miguel. "They sat in the *jardin*, looked at each other and said, 'Why did we go anyplace else? Why didn't we come here first?' And so they did come here, but they also went home for the summers. I would spend holidays here. I would come every Christmas and Easter. Eventually they gave up everything in Canada and came here full time, so I could spend my summers here too.

"By 1981 I was looking at escaping what was bothering me at home, which was seeing so many teenagers. I taught slow learners in high school. So many teenagers were so frustrated, so without hope, so without moral and ethical guidance, every one being absolutely governed by what they were buying all the time. That hurt as much as being tired out all the time from work."

She quit and left Canada and lived in San Miguel on less than $200 a month. Because of all her vacation visits to her parents there were no surprises. Changes that have happened since are less welcome. She does not look forward to the planned new Walmart subsidiary supermarket.

"But on the other hand, I remember being in San Miguel, and people would not plan a dinner party and then go shopping. They would go shopping to see what there was, and then plan their dinner party. There was no brown sugar in town for several months. There was no toothpaste in town for a year, because the company making the tubes--we didn't import anything in those days-- had gone out of business. You couldn't plan on anything.

"So often we had no milk in town at all. Today we're very spoiled. The newcomers coming in seem to have a fair amount of money because, of course, that's where San Miguel has gone. Where are we now, number nine on *Conde Nast's* best places to live in the world?"

One of the ways San Miguel has changed during her tenure is the wide availability of consumer goods. "You no longer see the girls in long skirts; the style to mimic is all American. The uniform is now jeans. But for me I much prefer to be kind of green, to be light on the way I use the resources of this earth. Mexico is still a country I can do that in. I am delighted to be allowed to live that way. I can walk everywhere."

In front of her house sits her 1982 Renault, which she uses only for excursions. Its age is evident; Mexico is not kind to cars. The grill is missing, but she tells me she has found another and the garage man is holding it for her, perhaps until she is ready to sell it. Then she can dress it up a bit.

She does not buy canned goods, and rarely anything frozen. She assumes that because most foods can be bought fresh, there are fewer chemicals finding their way into her groceries. This might be debated by some because Mexico does not stand at the forefront of the environmental or organic movements. But then, people don't come here for its cutting-edge attitudes.

As she spoke of her "green," small footprint lifestyle, I wondered whether it might not in some way be connected to her dislike of the often large footprint of Americans. Was it a Canadian perspective of their way of slopping over their borders, or taking up too much space on the 18 inch sidewalks of San Miguel? While there is clearly an intrinsic merit to her view, it has a political context as well.

She also does without the ease of "speaking in my own tongue, having to work out how I can ask for something with the words I know. I have to do without my closest friends, family connections. But it's also totally beautiful here, which for an artistic person is very important." In the room where we sit the walls are covered, gallery style, with dozens of oils and water colors. Some are by Anna herself, others by her mother, some by her grandfather, yet others by painters that she or her parents knew. They clearly connect her to the art colony of San Miguel, the two art schools and dozens of galleries.

Another important feature of Mexico's appeal is its family orientation. "Here you just have a fiesta, and you enjoy it thoroughly and you stop what you're doing. It's not like it was in Canada. I would buy a subscription to a symphony series, and there'd be four [concerts] through the winter. That would be my highlight, and I'd sit in the concert and I'd say, 'Is this what life's all about, is this all I'm working hard for? These few moments? I can hardly enjoy it.'

"Here I enjoy my life all the time, every day, in spite of frustrations. And the frustrations are our fault. We have great expectations. We expect the post office to have stamps. You think you haven't asked properly. Then you're frustrated because you can't mail the letter that's expected somewhere. A lot of our cultural problems are from our lifestyle before San Miguel and our expectations from our conditioning."

Initially she found herself involved in a number of volunteer activities, but in recent years she has wound that down. She spent four years volunteering at the English library and is still on the board of directors of the Twenty-Four Hour Society, the burial organization. The name comes from Mexican law stating that a person must be buried within twenty-four hours of dying.

"The town has a great reputation for creating trouble within nearly all the volunteer movements. The scuttlebutt is that people come to town, and they're little fish in big ponds at home, and they suddenly find they're in a littler pond and they want to be big fish there. Then people here volunteering start bossing other people around."

Then there is the poverty, thrown into sharp relief by the obvious wealth of many expatriates. Anna's small footprint is one way she deals with this. She is not ostentatious in her lifestyle, although she acknowledges paying some Canadian income tax. "I'm working to help at present a group called Let's Make a Better World. I give my maid a lot of help. I helped pay for her husband's funeral, I put two of her girls through school, I found help for a man in the rancho whose little girl was going to quit school at twelve because there was no more [government support for attending] school. He said he could feed her and clothe her, but he couldn't afford her bus fare. I said, 'done,' and so she went to school for another four years."

Her response to poverty is a one-case-at-a-time activism. She has stopped attending benefits because the ticket prices have gotten so high, to the point of starting to take her food budget.

Anna does not use the word "expatriate," seeing it as an American word. "Nonresident" is her choice as a Canadian living abroad. She also finds that it is impossible to keep up with events at home. "There is no Canadian news on any American station." Bringing Canadian magazines in was cost-prohibitive. The only time she can catch up is when she returns. She no longer returns to vote, not knowing much about the candidates anymore. Pondering this diminishing connection I asked her if she could see herself ever returning to Canada.

"Oh, no! I've got my little plot in the cemetery. I always had that plan, to stay here and live the rest of my life here. I'm not sure what it would take to overturn that; it would have to be a major problem with the government."

At times there are lesser irritants. One would be the long distance bus system. "I've got myself into a little bit of hot water; it wasn't *legally* hot, but I watched a movie, an American movie. Two GIs in Europe, and I looked around and I wondered why I was listening to all this horrible language, so loud, and so I went to the bus driver and I said, "Could you turn down the sound, because everybody else is reading the subtitles and I'm the only one hearing it. I said, 'it's profane, all it said was motherfucker the whole time.'

"So he said, 'No,' so I turned around and I stood in the aisle, and I yelled, in Spanish, *chinga tu madre, chinga tu madre*. And then I said, 'You are all making your children listen to that in English, that is all that movie is saying, and I want you to know it because he won't turn down the sound for me.' The Spanish translation for motherfucker [in the subtitles] was *Oh Heavens!*" Subsequent complaints to the bus line had no result.

As for whether Anna might be a little different from other Canadians in San Miguel, she admits she doesn't know many of them. "We're not quite as gregarious as Americans are. Maybe we're a little bit more independent, in a way."

If the Canadians don't seem to offer or need each other's support as much as Americans, she has more Mexican support. "I have my maid. She comes in and tells me if there's a fiesta, if somebody's died, and she's there if a government paper comes to the door and I have to do something about it.

"I would like to tell you about something that happened that surprised me, a false accusation by a woman around the corner who runs a cheesy little restaurant. Her son, who is seventeen, parked his car in front of my house one night. I don't know them from Adam, and I had gone out and come home to find a kind of a flutter, like the maid across the street was talking to me, and my maid was trying to talk to me. Suddenly there was this screaming woman, screaming at me about what I had done to her son's car. It turns out that somebody had thrown two rocks through his windshield and put a slice at least twelve inches long in each tire. Here she was saying that I had done it.

"I told her to get out of my house, because she'd come into the house, and she wouldn't leave, so I called the police. By the time the police came she'd left the house and they took different kinds of reports, probably from her, and it turned out that I was accused of doing that damage to that boy's car." Several days later she had to appear at the district attorney's office, and went with a friend to help her translate, which by then, she was too nervous to do herself. A lawyer was present, as was the boy and his mother. The lawyer opened by asking whether Anna intended to pay for the damage. She replied that she certainly was not going to pay, she had not damaged the car and knew nothing about it.

Under Mexican law, the mother had to prove that Anna had done it. She went up and down Jesus looking for witnesses. She was able to get a doctor and four other people to sign against her. When the papers were filed Anna was called back to the district attorney's office to respond to the evidence. She repeated again that she had nothing to do with the car damage and that she slept in the last of a string of six rooms, the room farthest from the street. She had heard nothing.

Surprisingly, the attorney asked if she would like him to handle her defense.

What emerged, in further questioning, was that the maid in the victim's family had overheard the boy tell his sister he got into an altercation with some friends and they had damaged his car. The boy's mother then dropped the charges.

In her final appearance at the district attorney's office, Anna said, "I'm sorry, that's not enough. I want an apology. So he pulls the lady in, because she happens to be in the building. She doesn't ever exactly apologize, so I say to the lawyer, 'Is this an apology?' So he says to the woman, 'get on with it.'

"And I said, 'Furthermore, I want you to go to each of the people you had sign against me and tell them that I'm innocent.' I guess the moral of my story is that, even though I'm not a native Mexican, the system was there for me, it was free, and it helped me even against a Mexican accuser. It proved to me that I could be here, and be safe, and be supported. You don't need a foreign community."

Although Anna found reasons in this event to be reassured about the legal process, I found it troubling in other ways. It made me wonder about the quality of some of her neighbors, not just the woman whose son suffered the car damage, but the four others plus the doctor who were willing to put their signatures on a piece of false testimony. And this was against a woman who had lived among them for years. Was there possibly a sense that the gringa might well have a lot of money and would pay for the damages rather than undergo the hassle of a legal battle? If so, they seriously misjudged Anna B. Even past seventy, and in a country not her own, she is not the type to duck a good scrap.

Social life, if you don't want to date, is fabulous, she says, "and a lot of the women here are very happy being single, independent women. Some of them are divorced, and some of them are like myself never married. There are lots of men to talk to on a friendly level. Nobody expects women to be escorted anymore in San Miguel, so that you can go as a single woman anywhere you want."

Still, she tries to return to Canada every year. Once there, she doesn't feel like returning immediately. "It's culture shock," she says. "I can drink the water, I can clean my teeth without looking for special water. I can speak English to everybody who's important. I have a good time in Canada, I get exhausted, and I miss, incredibly, rice and beans."

Her visits rarely involve using the Canadian health care system; she finds the facilities in San Miguel completely adequate. She can usually see the doctor the same day she calls, unlike at home, and the doctor still makes house calls.

She pays little attention to Mexican politics, feeling that it's not her role to be involved in it, and in a larger sense she would rather focus her interests in culture and archaeology.

Anna has friends among Mexicans as well as foreigners, something not everyone succeeds with. At times these interactions illustrate a great deal about Mexico. "I was invited to a family in La Esperanza and they were having a celebration for their son who had just graduated from university. They, as a family, make ceramics and I used their ceramics in my home.

"So I said, 'what time to come?' They said, 'Whenever you want.' 'It's a Sunday. Shall I come early?' 'Whenever you want.'" In the absence of more specific instructions, Anna had breakfast and left about ten o'clock, thinking to arrive about noon. On arrival, "There was absolutely nothing happening, but some people had gathered, and they offered us beer or Cokes. I was there for five hours with not a thing to eat. I saw a little lady making *tortillas*, and I went over and said, 'Please could I have one,' so I was given a *tortilla*.

"Finally we get to eat. There are no knives, no forks, no spoons, and the hunks of meat are put on the table for us to tear apart with *tortillas* in our hands. When it got dark there were *mariachis*, and I wondered was there going to be cake, or what was going to happen, because I was staying the night with them. There were about fifty or fifty people out in the yard. I went and had a little sleep in my car. When I came back I asked if it would be all right if I went to bed."

They said, "Certainly. Come on in the house."

"I don't know whose bed I took, but when I went to the bathroom I stepped over several members of the family, one who was sleeping in front of the bathroom door. And so the next day I was served a lovely breakfast and was reprimanded by my host for having eaten a *tortilla* without him offering it. I thought, I will *never* understand this country!"

This after twenty-five years.

CHAPTER 12

A BETTER BERKELEY

Augaust is part of the rainy season in San Miguel, something I used to think of as a modest squall moving through town two or three times a week in the late afternoon, clearing the dust from the cobblestones. This year it challenges the memory and the patience of even long time residents. The rains have been torrential. One day we had nearly four inches in an hour. We've had two hailstorms that shredded our bougainvillea. The hillside neighborhood next to us is moving south, literally, as with every storm my neighbors lose several square meters of real estate. It comes to rest in the intersection 50 feet below as a foot thick blanket of mud mixed with well-seasoned trash. This normally water-starved region is releasing water from the reservoir daily.

Twelve kilometers from us, near the village of Atotonilco, a widely-revered pilgrimage site that attracts visitors from all over Mexico, stands the eight acre spread of Susan Page and Mayer Shacter. The house is two tall stories with curving custom windows and ironwork and a rooftop observation post. It's red-violet color greets the eye like an exclamation point atop a gentle mound in what was once a pasture with more than a hundred gnarly mezquite trees. Fifty feet from the house, down a curving walkway sheltered from the weather, is Mayer's studio and gallery in a matching design. The Laja River, usually ten feet wide and six inches deep, is now 500 feet wide and twenty feet deep. Nearly half the property is under water. The house, ultramodern and deep fuchsia in color, topped at the high second story level by a platform for viewing the stars, now appears remote and moated. It's still a good effect and the owners are not disturbed. It is a site that seems peaceful and composed.

Mayer Shacter leans over the rail on the edge of the terrace and points to an area where the river ought to be. Now in his sixties, he is still trim and intense, with round steel glasses and short grizzled hair. My next question puts him back fifty years.

"I hitchhiked to South America when I was nineteen years old and at that time I really fell in love with Latin America. I subsequently made trips over the years back to Mexico. I had a fantasy in my head about this being where I wanted to live. If I had another lifetime I wanted to live it in Mexico. When I was sixty years old Susan and I were sitting in a restaurant in Cuernavaca talking. It was my birthday. We realized that we had enough things in place in our lives where we could actually make this happen.

"I had a successful business in the Bay Area selling mid-century modern [furniture and accessories]. We came down here during Christmas of 2001, to San Miguel and liked it, but we weren't really thinking of moving down here at that time."

The following year they came back at the same time, but stayed for six weeks, visiting a wider group of towns. "On that trip," Mayer continues, "we started to look at land wherever we went. The clincher for us was when we came back to San Miguel at the end of that trip and decided to just check out real estate here. I realized very quickly that if we were to buy real estate I didn't want to live in town. It was too crowded for me. I had lived in the country in the 60s. We asked the real estate guy to show us some country land. What really sold us was finding this piece of land, this eight acres out here, on the river, with two existing buildings. We made an offer on it the next day."

The two buildings on the property were from the 80s, nothing historic. One was a rattan furniture factory, the other a warehouse. They stood about fifty feet apart. When planning their home and studio, the architects were able to incorporate all the beams and roof structure as well as the existing footprint.

"We're fifteen minutes from town," says Mayer, "but we could be a hundred miles from town. It feels re-mote but it isn't remote."

After the deal was made, they returned to Berke-ley and discussed what would happen next. Having bought the land seemed to accelerate the process, giving a specific focus to their dream. Sooner looked better than later. Mayer liquidated his business in four weeks. They sold their house and two other properties in San Francisco and in seven months they were back. It was the beginning of September, 2003 and the process had been driven by Mayer. How was it affecting Susan?

"It was a more difficult transition for me," she says. "We had those two commercial properties, and we had recently paid them off. I think it's an element in a lot of people's stories that real estate is what enabled them to do this. That was what got us thinking that maybe we could do something different. Both of us wanted to be in the country. Both of us had fantasized having land and a pond." When they began site preparation for their new home, the pond was the first feature to go in.

But the fantasy for Susan had never been centered in Mexico. They had both lived in Berkeley for more than thirty years, but as far as having land and a pond, "You couldn't come up with that combination in Berkeley. You'd have to drive three hours to get it. This property was the combination we'd been looking for, and that's what got me started thinking. I hadn't thought it would be in Mexico, but maybe I *should* think about that.

"As we were driving back up to Berkeley we were talking about having a five-year plan, a ten-year plan, because I wasn't ready to move, to make that transition so fast. When we got back I went through these emotional wrenches because I believed there were three very compelling reasons for us to do this. Number one, Mayer could retire. Two, we could build our dream house. [Three] Mayer said to me, 'You could live your life out, here in Berkeley, and you know what that would be like, or we could add a whole new adventure to our lives.' That was very compelling for me.

"I was always behind the project, but I did have feelings of grief and loss. I would be sitting in a restaurant or waiting for a movie to begin and just start crying, [thinking], oh, am I really going to do this? We went from a five-year plan to a seven-month plan pretty quickly. I had some feelings about that, but I was never ambivalent about [ultimately] doing it."

At the time they moved Susan had just completed a book project, and during the first year in San Miguel she founded the Author's Sala, an organization that brings in and showcases the talents of popular authors. One of the early guests was Alan Rinzler, who had edited Toni Morrison, Shirley MacLaine, Robert Ludlum, Hunter Thompson and others. At the end of the week he and Susan had a conversation about what she'd been doing. "He was interested in my work, and I ran a project past him and he read the proposal on the airplane on the way home. As soon as he landed he called me back and said, 'I want you to do this book.' So I wrote my last book while we were renting in Independencia [as their house was being constructed]." This book, titled *Why Talking Is Not Enough*, is her sixth. Her previous books have been translated into twenty-two languages. Of course, Spanish is one of them.

Susan herself does not speak much Spanish after five years and regrets that she hasn't done more to learn it. Mayer started trying to pick up Spanish on his first trip. He now has enough to do business easily, but doesn't call himself fluent. "Functional" is the word he uses. Still, it made the twenty-two months of construction that began in January of 2004 much easier.

"We had a major ground breaking ceremony," says Susan. "We had a shaman come and we buried salt to add spice to life and coins to offer prosperity. We buried a Virgin of Guadalupe and a little bone our dog, who had died, had worn all his life."

We are sitting now in Susan's office, where her high built-in workstation projects into the room like a cockpit in the prow of a ship. It points firmly in the direction of the growing flood plain outside, suggesting

foresight. Beside me are shelves of her books in a variety
of languages. Relationships among couples are what she
writes about, but it's clear that their relationship to the
land, to its people and its culture is what informs their
lives.

Out at the edge of the water two brilliantly white
egrets walk slowly over the flooded meadow, looking
downward intently, hopefully. I'm not sure they're going
to find much.

"The people are wonderful," says Mayer.
"They're very good natured, kind, and friendly. I'm an
aficionado of Mexican folk art. You couldn't be in a better place than Mexico right now. Some of the best work
that's ever been done is being done here right now. We've
developed relationships with many different craftspeople.
We travel throughout Mexico to buy things. It connects
us to Mexican culture in a way that most people never
experience here."

Susan's emotional difficulties about the move dis-
solved over the first year as she became deeply involved
in setting up the Authors' Sala. "What I caught myself
saying once, and I've repeated now many times, is that it's
more of what I loved about Berkeley than Berkeley. What
I loved there was the sense of community and the sense
that I lived among people who were like-minded. What is
important to me is a feeling of belonging and having close
friends. Here in San Miguel what I love so much is that we
all know each other."

I bring up the idea that there may be cliques or
strata here. They both quickly reject the idea that they
belong to the golf set, the Young Republicans, or the
cocktail set. "I'm very involved with the musical groups

here," adds Susan. "The opera, the chamber music, the Pro Musica, And of course, the Authors' Sala and the Literary Society, which I started." She feels that, unlike these cliques, most of the groups they are involved with overlap a great deal. "When somebody gives a party we are probably going to know at least three-quarters of the people there."

Moving to Mexico was in no way an escape. They loved their lives in Berkeley, and if they were forced to leave Mexico for reason of revolution or upheaval, they would return to Berkeley. They are here because of what Mexico is, rather than what it isn't.

"I've always done work that I enjoyed very much," says Mayer, "things that fulfilled me. I was a studio ceramic artist, I renovated homes in the Bay Area, I was an owner-builder, I've been in the antiques business for many years and I've loved everything I've ever done. There's nothing we were fleeing there. We were coming for this new experience. Being involved with the different artisans is helping to keep the patrimony alive. So many have fallen by the wayside through the change in culture, kids being able to go to the university who never were able to before. Customs changing, imports from China, all of those things have affected folk art in Mexico.

"For the most part, the folk art that I'm selling is not the typical trinkets you find in the artisan markets in town. I've paid as much as a thousand dollars for a piece. These things are folk art, yet they transcend folk art at the same time. The fact that the people I'm working with can make a good living helps to keep the crafts alive."

The Mexican connection runs very deep with them, but what about their ongoing connection to the

States? Is it a trade off or can they coexist? Mayer responds first. "I go back to the States for ten days or two weeks once a year to see my grand kids and my son and daughter-in-law and a few friends. That's more than enough for me. I'd rather be here. I find when I travel in the United States today a certain sameness everywhere. Everywhere you go there are big sprawling malls. All of the individuality of the United States with the exception of New York City, Santa Fe, San Francisco—there are these unique enclaves. Even Berkeley has flattened out over the years. I mean, all of the individual booksellers, most of them are gone now. I find myself just bored there. My life here feels so much richer and fuller. It's a struggle for me to go back every year to see everybody.

"Mexico is a first world *and* a third world country today. It's modernizing rapidly and the economy seems to be growing. There's very little you give up today by coming to Mexico. We have satellite TV and we watched the Democratic Convention and we watched the Olympics. We're part of a new culture, but we're not really estranged from our old one."

"I come out a little bit different from Mayer on this," says Susan. "I love going back up to the States. The [trips] are getting less frequent, but [I go] twice or three times a year. I miss the lawns and the lush scenery of New England and Pennsylvania and Ohio. I like to go back there; it restores my soul. I plan trips whenever I can, but the dilemma is I'm always missing something down here. It's a trade off."

A question about Mexican friends evokes a familiar story. "We have Mexican friends," says Mayer, "but it's a long slow process. They have to speak English; it's harder to develop a friendship when you're not fluent in the language. We have people whom we're friendly with, that we invite over for a party, but it's not the same as the expat community. That really surprised me. I thought we would have more Mexican friends."

Yet they are hard put to think of anything that would make them return to the U.S. short of a revolution that confiscated their property. "I think Mexico is way beyond that," he says. But if that did happen, they'd return to Berkeley.

"We weren't itching to get out of Berkeley when we retired," says Susan. "I always fantasized retiring in Berkeley and having more time to do more of the things I loved to do there."

"We traveled a lot. We've been to Asia and Europe and many other places. There's just no other place I'd rather be," adds Mayer. "Mexico has this incredible combination of being close to the United States, but so far away at the same time. And it's exotic and gritty and so different from anything we ever experience in the United States. I pinch myself practically every day that it has come to pass that we're living here.

"People always ask us about health care. I've had some of the best health care of my life here in Mexico. There is a quality of caring that doesn't exist anymore in the United States because of all the managed health care. There's the best dentist I've ever had in my life; we have a wonderful internist here. I've experienced a lot of generosity and kindness here, gentleness. I look forward to going to the dentist.

"Recently when Tom Robbins was down here for this literary event he was talking about both teeth and eye operations he'd had in the U.S. and how they were both botched. That can happen anywhere in the world, but generally I feel very comfortable with all that health care here in Mexico."

Mayer begins recalling how his antiques store was in an area of largely Mexican businesses in east Oakland, and what a hard working and mutually supportive community it was.

"The contrast between poverty in Mexico and poverty in the United States is quite striking, because it's in your face in both places much of the time, but you don't see homelessness here. You did see it no matter where you went in the U.S. Here people have enough to eat, there's family to surround them, and it's rare that you see anybody that's so destitute that they're sleeping on the street, even in Mexico City."

"Here the families take care of each other," adds Susan.

Even when they had to dig a bit, most people I've talked to here acknowledge that they've changed since they came. Sometimes it's so gradual it's hard to see. Some people see it best when they return to the States for a visit. Mayer finds a kind of nonlinear continuity in his life that makes this change seem not very different from what went before. "I've been an oddball all my life and I've found ways to live my life the way I thought it should be lived. For me this is just one more adventure that I've had, and you bring yourself along wherever you go. I didn't go to university, I didn't have a corporate job. This is kind of in the whole stream of life that I've lived. For me, I'm just having a great time. I never bought into patriotism, I have always felt more like a citizen of the world. People talk about their soul and where they feel comfortable. This is where my soul resides. I feel at home here in a way that I've never felt at home anywhere else in my life. Everywhere I go I see beauty here."

"I would just add that I have heard people comment about Mayer that he is more relaxed here," says Susan.

"I didn't plan on opening the gallery. We had a very different vision of how our lives would be here. I love having the gallery; it's like what I've always done. I commute 15 seconds to work. I'm open when I'm here."

"And we're not dependent on the gallery for income," says Susan, "so it's not stressful. I didn't know what *I* was going to do when we first came down, and I remember the first year thinking, well this is fun, this is nice to go to town all the time and have coffee with my friends but I don't want to live my whole life on vacation. I'm not ready to retire yet. Then the opportunity came up to write this other book, so I did that. There was a certain amount of promotion for the book and I was caught up in that.

"So I kept thinking, what am I going to do when I have some choices? One day I woke up, and I had started this organization, the Authors' Sala, and that's what I've done all my life. I was a campus minister, and I worked in non-profits. I founded a battered women's shelter. When I came down here I saw a vacuum and started an organization to fill it. I just completed one of the biggest projects I probably ever put together, the summer literary festival featuring Tom Robbins. And I loved it! There really wasn't much time that was stressful, but mostly I love to do this. I had a wonderful team of collaborative volunteers.

The best part of what I love to do is recruit and train and support volunteers."

Susan Page wonders occasionally whether she ought to put her hand to something else if she ever stops doing this. What about painting? She's never painted, but there is that feeling of possibility. "It turns out that I'd already discovered those things I liked to do, and it has turned out that I'm still doing those things. So I don't think I've changed very much."

I wonder aloud whether the future looks much different. Neither can see any changes except those brought on by aging. In a few days or perhaps a couple of weeks the river will recede. The egrets will move on. The meadow and pond will resume their normal look with a burro tethered at one side. Mayer will collect and deal and Susan will manage her volunteers. She will plan the next literary event. They will continue to travel, both in Mexico and elsewhere.

"The future has arrived," says Susan. "It's here. We always wanted to create a home where we could display our artwork. There's a certain satisfaction in achieving goals that you've had all your life."

The house was built as a showcase for their collections. One has the feeling that the very best folk art pieces from the gallery often come into the house, at least for a time. In one cabinet in the great room are dozens of pieces of Mayer's own work, tea pots of great whimsy that seem constructed of mechanical or plumbing components, yet all are formed of clay. Throughout the rooms most surfaces display a huge variety of pieces, many of them of museum quality. Don't stumble, I remind myself.

"I may or may not do some more writing," she

adds. "I'm going to leave that up to serendipity."

"When Susan and I met, we were basically impoverished. I had been living in a cult for six years. I came out of that literally with $80 in my pocket. I owned nothing. I had to start my life over again at the age of thirty-seven."

"I had just left," says Susan, "the last job I ever had working for someone else. I had left that to devote myself to writing. I was a starving writer, he was a starving artist."

"What I want to say," adds Mayer, "is that having lived my life the way I have by following my passions most of my life, I never made much money. I always had a lot of 'psychic pay.' The only reason all of this became possible is because I bought these properties in the Bay Area in ghetto areas and renovated them, and everything changed in twenty-five years. I've always had good taste but I've never had the means to realize some of the fantasies in my head. All of this is kind of a cosmic joke to me. People come here, and they've never seen anything like this in their lives. I never had corporate bonuses or anything like that. Had I bought those properties in Buffalo, New York, I'd still be living in Buffalo, New York."

"I think what he's trying to convey," Susan adds, "is that we wake up with a sense of awe every morning. We were forty-three when we bought our first property. We were both busy being countercultural hippies and with political involvement in our 30s. We had never bought property; we had never settled down. We had a lot of catching up to do. The fact that we're here is just a miracle to us."

"There was a day when Susan said to me, talking about real estate, 'We're doomed. All of our friends own property. We're in our 40s and we have nothing.' And flash forward, and here we are. It's a joke how things have played out." Mayer laughs and shakes his head as if the irony lingers.

"I think both of us feel this," Mayer continues. "I really, in my younger years, struggled to find myself, and I had a certain amount of help from my parents. The only thing that I miss is calling up Mom on the phone, or having her come for a visit to enjoy this."

But Mayer's mother is not alive to see his achievement and it becomes an emotional moment for him to think about it. "That's the only thing," he says when he's able to speak again.

"In the last six years," says Susan, "we lost his mother and both my parents." None of their parents ever saw this property, although Susan's mother had seen the plans for the house and was very excited about the project. Susan herself grew up on a three-acre plot in Ohio where her father did experimental horticulture for the state. That early sense of space explains why she now finds the property here so fulfilling. "He would have been happy that we are doing this. He would have loved to come here, and it is sad that it all happened after he died."

For Mayer it evokes a time in the 1960s when he was part of a group that owned 160 acres on the Mendocino coast. There he raised livestock and had a huge organic garden. "I also had it in my head to have a piece of land again. I had that experience and I had the experience of living in the city and having neighbors up against you. The dogs would be barking and neighbor would be yelling, 'Shut up!' In San Miguel de Allende, you don't only have neighbors twenty-five feet away, they're up against your wall. I have no interest in living that way again. Having some space around us where we can walk outside naked is incredible."

I take this to mean that if you're planning a visit, you ought to call first.

Final words?

"There's such an abundance here," says Susan. "So much more of what I love about life here than what I ever had before."

"It's either that your glass is half full or half empty," adds Mayer, "and the people I've seen leave here, their lives have been half empty lives. They leave for reasons like they can't get *The New York Times* every day on their doorstep. They came here for the wrong reasons. They didn't come here because they loved Latin American culture, they came here because life might be less expensive. If you come here for the wrong reasons you're not going to be happy in Mexico."

"I feel like we have more friends here who are happy couples," says Susan after a moment of reflection. "They feel they've lived a rich life together, they know how to get along with each other, and that wasn't so true in the States. It seemed like there were a lot of troubled couples, couples who couldn't pull it together and were always on the verge of leaving each other. It seems like either this place attracts couples who know how to get along with each other and are very happy together or this environment engenders that sort of thing."

"The other thing for me," adds Mayer, "is the number of truly creative people who've done interesting things in their lives, that have ended up here. This is kind of a self-selecting location. We have so many friends who've had such rich and full lives, and they bring those experiences down to San Miguel and end up contributing to the community in various ways."

Afterwards Mayer holds an umbrella over my head as we walk out to my car, parked at the edge of the gallery. It begins to rain hard again, the water streaming down the curved windows and parapets of the house, over the undulating ironwork. The vivid colors are more intense when they're wet. The river will be creeping closer to the pool now, and the burro is moving to higher ground.

CHAPTER 13

THE GIRLFRIEND

I'm done performing," says actor Cynthia Simmons. "I would prefer to do some writing now. But I liked the stage, and I liked repertory. There were not a lot of people doing repertory by the time I got to New York, but there were some. There was one uptown, it was called the 127th St. Repertory Ensemble. I loved working there because when they put their season together two or three times a year, there were always three or four plays running in rep. That was a great experience."

We are sitting in her living room in the San Antonio neighborhood, where she has recently moved. Boxes still line the walls. Her art is hung, but there's much more to do. Behind her a Katrina figure, four feet tall, stands against a corner wall, cigarette holder extended. A skeletal persona in dramatic dress, she looks about to declaim a line from Shakespeare or Shaw. As does Cynthia herself, whose gestures are still exact and refined. But then, as she said, she's done performing now.

Cynthia is a petite black woman of fifty-eight with a ponytail of graying dreadlocks and a voice with the timbre of old mahogany. In her later career in New York she was known as the author and actor in *Sally Hemings in the White House,* a one-woman play she wrote as a vehicle for herself.

Sally Hemings was a slave owned by Thomas Jefferson's wife, who died in childbirth in 1783. Sally, a light skinned woman who could pass for white, accompanied Jefferson to Paris where she looked after four surviving daughters, and later became his mistress. It is not clear how many children they had together. Although reports of the relationship emerged in the mudslinging presidential campaigns of the early nineteenth century, it was later nearly forgotten and the story was only a whisper for decades, until in the 90s DNA testing proved it true. The thing I did not know before, the thing that convinced me I had to talk to Cynthia Simmons, was that Sally Hemings and Thomas Jefferson's wife had the same father. This gave the story an entirely different spin.

"Everything in the professional theater is type, and the type that I was, I wasn't being asked to do a lot of things that were interesting."

"What type was that?"

"I was the girlfriend. They definitely were not buying interesting girlfriends for whatever black characters were being written. One of my friends did a one-woman show on Harriet Tubman. It got her performances other times of the year, but she could pretty much work every night in February, for black history month. She could actually make enough money in February to live maybe for four or five months, if she would hustle.

"So I got started looking for a character. One of my friends suggested Sally Hemings, and I really didn't know that much about her. When I started researching, it was such an interesting story, but what I hadn't thought about was that Sally Hemings was never Harriet Tubman, someone who would go down easy for white America. I did get a chance to work with it a lot [on stage], but it was never something that I could go out with every night, because so many people didn't want to believe it."

At a more interesting level, this was another girl-friend role, and since Jefferson was the first president to occupy the nearly finished White House, it made Sally Hemings the first African American woman to occupy the presidential suite.

I raise the question of whether that very aspect of it, the controversy, might not have given it wings. Think of *Hair.*

"What was interesting to me was that people still had such strong reactions to the concept of Jefferson having a relationship with a woman for thirty-eight years, and she wasn't all white. It amazed me that people could think that diminished him. It was just another part of who he was. There was a lot of resistance. I guess controversy can be good, but it depends on what icons you're stepping on.

"Race is still America's Achilles heel. That's one of the reasons why this election was so interesting, because I don't think of Obama as African American. I think of him as of African descent. I think the fact that he is not a product of slave descendants made this easier. He's biracial. He didn't grow up in an African American home, he grew up in a white household. He's a really interesting choice. I don't think any African Americans, if we thought about or fantasized about a black president, would have thought about it being someone of Obama's background."

I ask who she might have picked in his place,

but she comes up with no one. It's not an easy question, and for many people, Obama's victory is still a considerable surprise. "I wouldn't want to replace him. I just don't know why anybody would want to be president right now."

No argument there.

❂❂❂

Cynthia had heard about San Miguel for years before she visited the first time but it was not until she met a Mexican American woman in a master's program who had done her senior year in high school in San Miguel, that it sounded like a place she had to see for herself. This was in June of 2004. "Two friends and I came down here, but we also went to Ajijic. One of the women I was traveling with was considering retirement in Mexico. We thought that we would like Ajijic better than San Miguel because it was near Guadalajara, the big city, and we were all from New York. But we didn't much care for it. We didn't really like the Americans that we met. They just weren't our tribe. There's nothing wrong with them, but they weren't the people we saw ourselves hanging out with. We cut short our stay and came to San Miguel."

It was not her intention to move to San Miguel at that point; she had just moved to New Orleans. But on returning she lost her house to hurricane Katrina, and since the friend she might normally have stayed with in Atlanta had just taken a job in London, she came back to Mexico. She was looking for a healing space after the storm.

"This was in 2005. It was what I could afford. I'm doing some grant writing [now], survival writing, but not so much personal. I work for organizations in the States, not-for-profits, and help them raise money."

Did she speak any Spanish at the time she moved?

"In San Miguel you don't have to speak Spanish, but that limits who you can talk to. This is a town where people have been here for fifteen years and they just barely get by in Spanish."

Getting here she found little that surprised her. "It was beautiful, it was a feast for the senses, it was easy to navigate. Being a New Yorker I didn't want to drive. That was one of the reasons I liked New Orleans. They have great buses and it's really small. You do not have to drive everywhere, and I'm really averse to that."

Katrina had left her with a lot of anger and the need to work it out. It was not only the mindless violence of the storm itself, it was even more the perceived racist overtones in the way the aftermath was handled by the authorities. "It was them using it as a way to completely change the demographics in New Orleans."

It's story I'd like to hear, but it's not a San Miguel story.

"That's one of the things that other people of color who have been here for a while have talked about. It's how the issues that can just make you want to shoot somebody in the States are not issues here. There is no race issue with Mexicans. How can there be an issue with color in Mexico? It's just what your lineage is. The rhythm of Mexico—even though the people of Spanish descent may have a lot of influence [here]—the Indian rhythm is what is the pace of this country, not European. It's not that race may not be an issue with some of the white people who have settled here, but it's not an issue with Mexico.

"Most of Europe has some kind of racism because most European countries colonized either some
part of Africa or the Caribbean. But once you get out of
that environment you are acutely aware that the world is
colored. The world is not white. Americans think that the
world is white because of where they travel. Years ago I
was working in one of the investment banks, and we were
in the smoking room and we were talking about being a
minority. One white woman talking to me said, talking
about the shifting demographics in New York, 'Well, Cynthia, no one wants to be a minority,' and I said, 'You always have been, you just don't go anywhere, so you don't
know that.' It's different once you get out of European-
based society."

I bring up one of the threads in these conversations, whether she is here because of what Mexico is or
isn't. Although it isn't a place that has the racial issues that
run just below the surface as in the U.S., the stratification
here is clear, and the climate is different. It is as if among
Mexicans there's a continuum of color, from white to very
dark. In America you're white or black, but I wouldn't
characterize Mexico as a place with no race issue. It's
there but differently cast.

"It's both," she says. "I had a friend who spent
four or five years living in Jamaica. During that time, because I had no place to stay and the [exchange rate] was
fabulous, I was there every time I could figure out a ticket.
What I realized was that life was much more comfortable
in places where it was simpler. Where people weren't so
tied into, 'I gotta have this, I gotta have that.' There is very
little that any of us do that is life-sustaining. Outside of
that it really doesn't matter whether it gets done today or

tomorrow. But you have to be in a culture that isn't always now, now, now.

"Living there let me understand that I needed to live in a place for a time that was simpler, where people's ideas and expectations about life were to me more honest. I think I had always thought I would do that in Jamaica, but I had an illness that allowed me to start looking at other things about a place. If you get sick in Jamaica what people are trying to do is get to the States. Mexico has world-class hospitals. Part of it is what it isn't, but part of it is what it is.

"It was also to be in a place where I'm not race-identified. It was easier to explore other dimensions, because none of us is just one thing. Growing up as a person of color in the States, that becomes more dominant than anything else that you are. It's like the women's movement. That was interesting, but I was African American way before. Also, so many of the issues of the women's movement were not black women's issues because we had always worked. We had to work.

"Once I started to travel I realized that a big part of America's problem was its youth. It's a baby country. The first time I went to Europe I was amazed at how much more polite people were." I point out that the same is true of Mexico. Manners count. The sense of *cortesia* is real and alive. "We just never got refined there in a lot of ways," she says, nodding. "I find much more of it in the South than I do anywhere else [there]. The fact that people speak to you in neighborhoods."

Being part of the neighborhood in San Miguel, however, presents other obstacles. Cynthia is not certain how she fits. "There are things about the culture that I want to study, but it's sort of specific. I'm really interested in the crafts. My mother was a visual artist. I want to do a lot more of that, but the first year I was here I don't know that I was involved with San Miguel at all, because every six or eight weeks I went back to New Orleans to work on my house. It was just somewhere to be. What I do find here that is very easy is figuring out community. People are very friendly."

Cynthia's initial connections were through her Yoga classes, and then through a book club. Does she have Mexican friends?

"Oh yes, but not a lot because my Spanish still sucks. But I think it's just who you're fortunate enough to meet. The woman that I'm close with was married to an Englishman and so lived abroad for a long time. She's lived somewhere outside of here. It's just a different conversation that you have with someone who better understands the world that you have inhabited before you came here."

Unlike most people in these conversations Cynthia is still working.

"My situation is a little different. Most people who came down here came as retirees. I'm not that." She's largely supported here by her grant writing, which doesn't provide a lot of surplus. Her dining out is more often done at the homes of friends rather than restaurants. Responding to a question about social life for a single person here, she says, "San Miguel doesn't provide a lot of social life. It depends on what your interests are. The things that engage me the most in the States are either not here, or not in the way that I appreciate them. The big music thing here is chamber music. I don't like it, I like jazz. Jazz here sucks."

Perhaps she's been involved in theater things here, given her history.

"Oh God, no! Way too amateurish. And I'm not trying to do that anymore."

So is she more involved with the States? For her first year in San Miguel, definitely. But it was more specifically connected with the aftermath of Katrina in New Orleans. More recently she's been tracking the campaign and election of 2008.

"I probably go home [to New York] a couple of times a year, but each year it gets less frequent. That has more to do with the fact that I don't have a lot of money and I would prefer to continue seeing parts of the world I haven't visited, rather than keep going back to the parts that I know. Especially since you cannot buy the cheap tickets anymore."

None of this translates into certainty about staying in San Miguel. The future is unclear. If she had a windfall she might return to the States. "If I had to work to maintain a lifestyle in the States that I enjoy, I'm not doin' that. I'm not ever working sixty hours a week again."

Unlike some, her time in San Miguel has not changed her view of the U.S. "I don't think I ever thought of the States as home. I never knew where home was, never had a clue. But if it's home they're supposed to treat you good, and I didn't come up in a time when they treated African Americans well in the States, so how could that be home? So I've always felt homeless. I have not been to that place in the States that was home."

The idea of homelessness brings up the vast differences in means here. "Poverty is much less extreme in places where you don't have severe winter, where you can still pick food off the trees, and especially places that are near the water so you can also bathe. In Jamaica that was one of the things I was amazed at. A bum's life in Jamaica just didn't seem that bad to me."

I raise the point that Mexico, without an extensive government welfare safety net on the style of the U.S., still has the original prototype safety net, the family. "I think it's also the form of safety net that most Americans, too, relied on until maybe the fifties. It took till my generation for anyone in my family to avail themselves of social welfare programs if circumstances changed. It just wasn't what you did. If you didn't have a job you let the matriarch of the family know, and everybody put whatever they could in an envelope and mailed it to you every week. By the time we got to my generation the living patterns were different. I think the thing that I did most was unemployment, being an actor. But my mom's generation, I don't remember any of them going outside of family during hard times."

Cynthia's apartment sits on a modest street. From my place on the sofa I can look through the dining room into a garden behind. It's the kind of apartment that is not expensive in San Miguel, although it's comfortable, secure and well maintained. There's not much traffic outside, so it's also quiet. Does she find this town an inexpensive place to live?

"It is, although it depends on how and where you live. I don't know that I could buy a house here, but it costs me a third of what it would cost me to live in New York, which was the last place I lived, in a huge studio, and half of what it would cost in New Orleans."

Would she live in New York again if she could?

"I think if I had money I might try San Francisco. I like the West Coast and I never have experienced the Bay Area. But I don't think that San Miguel is in any way typical of Mexico. For the last forty-five years the American presence has had an enormous influence on San Miguel. When I talk to Mexicans who live and work here, they think that's a good thing, because there's work here."

Leaving Cynthia Simmons, I take with me the sense of a different sort of conversation, one tilted more than a few degrees toward the differing racial overtones of both the U.S. and Mexico. Her views on the election of Barack Obama introduce a thought that has never occurred to me, that it lacks the element of expiation because he was not descended from slaves. Being of African descent is not enough, it does not complete the circle.

CHAPTER 14

CROSSING OVER

There's a blue house on a narrow street with nine-inch sidewalks near the Mercado Ramirez, the main fruit and vegetable market. The color reminds me of Frida Kahlo's house in Mexico City. Like most of the houses here, the facade doesn't give much away.

Inside, Caren and Dave Cross have given more thought to understanding and articulating the San Miguel experience than anyone I know. Caren is the producer/director of *Lost and Found in Mexico*, an award-winning documentary that frames the feelings and insights of other expatriates within her own startling life-changing experience. The title says it all.

Initially I thought I would not talk to the Crosses. After all, they had said what they wanted to say, and said it passionately and well. I owned a copy of their film, and I knew that what I wanted to do was sufficiently different that we need not cross paths. I also did not want to appear to be replicating Caren's effort.

But the more people I talked to about their San Miguel experience, the more imperative it became to talk with them. For one thing, the film had mostly been shot in

2003. Five years had passed and people's views evolve. I suspected that theirs had as well. It seemed as if I couldn't ignore their current perspective, since the film version had been so thoroughly grounded.

The Crosses first came to San Miguel for a ten-day visit in 1997. The film suggests that it was during this visit that Caren abruptly realized she could not continue with her present life in Virginia. There was no solution but to return and dismantle it. But this is a compression of the real events. The first ten-day trip planted real doubts about what she was doing and led to a second, six-week trip the following year.

"The last day of that six week trip we bought this house," says Caren. "During that six weeks it went from, 'Let's rent something for a month, two months, three months for next year.' It kept changing. It changed very fast."

"I used to walk a lot," adds Dave, unwinding onto a sofa opposite on the second floor terrace. His salt and pepper hair and beard are closely trimmed. "I showed Caren these streets. There was a lady who had a little three by five card on the door. We made arrangements that day to buy the house just before we went back. Then the idea was that we would fix it up and come six weeks every year, and between that March and the following September we went from six weeks to maybe eight weeks, then half the year till she sold her practice [she was a clinical social worker] to her partners and moved out. By September we were down here."

The walls of the terrace are painted the color of Granny Smith apples. Viewed through a double arch of *cantera* stone, the garden below holds a tile-lined fountain.

Opposite is Caren's painting studio where the film was edited. Thinking about how it took a year to reach that point, she says, "I don't think it got into me that we could really give up our lives until the next year."

Caren is not the only person in these conversations to have the idea of moving to San Miguel come to her as an unexpected imperative--the falling-off-the-cliff experience. It's always made me wonder what happens to the spouse in those situations. In the film Dave describes his move as "kind of an arranged marriage, one that worked out well." I had been left wanting to hear more about this, but the film had been cut from the 120 hours of footage shot to fifty-three minutes running time. It sounded like an endless string of tough choices.

Dave takes up the narrative. "We had been living in Virginia, which neither of us liked, for eighteen years. A beautiful place, Virginia Beach, but not our cup of tea. I had stopped working a couple years before that and had made a couple of trips looking for places. Where would be a better fit? Canada? West Coast? Minnesota? Nothing comes of it and the next year I did the same thing. Then we had this trip and Caren wants to come back. "I said, 'Look, I made you go to Virginia with me. Wherever you want to go, I'll go."

"Here are the words he said," adds Caren, "'I took us to Virginia, so it's your turn. I owe it to you."

"It wasn't like I hated it in Virginia'" says Dave. "Part of the things I liked about driving around the States was that it was an adventure. Ten years ago it was even more an adventure to live here in San Miguel, so that attracted me."

"This was 1998," says Caren.

I am thinking of their escape from Virginia. In the film Caren speaks to her background, and how she was always held to a higher standard, even as a kid. How did that play out as she wound down her practice? Didn't she feel heavily obligated to her clients in that same way?

"I had five months preparation to do that and it worked out fine."

"This was when insurance stuff really changed," adds Dave. "Clients who used to come for a year or 18 months or two years or five years were getting six visits and then they had to reapply. Therapy started not being what it used to be."

"In 1980," says Caren, "you'd say, this was what the client needed and you'd sign your name, and the amount of time needed to do paperwork was less than 1% of my time. Then it became 50% of my time. So for every hour I spent with a client there was an hour of writing stupid reports. It became tiresome, but I still thought I'd do it until I was eighty. I still loved it, the work itself."

I suggest that people who have the falling-off-the-cliff experience also have a lot of baggage, perhaps without being aware of it. Was this the case?

"Let me go back for a moment. I think when we came for the ten days, that wasn't falling off the cliff, that was, 'I love it here and I want to come back.' The falling was the next year, the six-week trip. That started things rolling."

What I see in this is that the high expectations aren't going to be met anymore. They're part of the baggage. The next thing was, how do you actually make this happen?

"Two answers" she continues. "One is I found

that most of us that made this move found somebody who became a mentor. It might be someone you meet on the street. Because it's hard, doing this. You're only fifty years old. How did you do this? How are you pulling this off? Are you worried about health insurance? I think most people find somebody that becomes a mentor. And then you start to realize, Oh my God, I *can* get out of this rut. It opens the door to, ah, that's how you do it! And these people look really happy here."

But Dave knows there are pitfalls. "One of the differences is this: many people go on vacations every year of their lives and every place they look at real estate and think, for example, 'Oh God, I want to live in Key West.'"

"Dave and I were always in realtors' offices."

Dave continues, "Then you realize Key West is 120 degrees in the summer. You can't stand the heat and it's too much rain. You get to the practicalities of it. If you're overseas you realize, gee, I'm away from everybody, I don't know the language. People come here—and I'll include us in this—and you meet people, and because they are expats themselves they're pretty open to you. You sit down in a restaurant and you're going to end up talking to people. You end up thinking, this isn't *like* anyplace else. It's very foreign, yet it has all this stuff that you know. People have already done this. It's been going on for years, it wasn't like we were reinventing anything. We were reinventing ourselves, maybe."

But they had no Spanish. David had studied Latin and French. Caren had some French and Italian.

"So," he continues, "it made it that much easier. People had already gotten things going. Someone is showing movies at the *Biblioteca*. There's like a safety net in a foreign place. If you felt like you were in trouble or you needed something, there's somebody here."

The film suggests that for Caren their move had initially been about what Mexico wasn't. It was more about the demands and the baggage falling away. She speaks about her life up to that point being much like a checklist. About doing well in high school to get into the right college, then the right grad school. Marrying the right guy and having the right kids and buying the right house. With each of these mileposts she could check something off, but the checklist did not accompany her across the border.

I ask if it has now become more about what Mexico *is*.

"I think for me the answer would be that it was about both equally. It was exotic and beautiful and color-ful and I loved the light." She looks at Dave. "For you? You just came along."

But then Dave was not unloading baggage in the way that Caren was. His career had gone from nuclear en-gineering to structural steel for the construction industry.

"I had stopped work and gone through some real personal [questions], like who am I, if I'm not doing any-thing, what am I? Coming down here had some sense of adventure and oddness to it, which it seems to have less of right now. I wasn't a person who knew anything about Mexican culture. I had no interest in it whatsoever. I thought that the beaches were gorgeous. When I first saw *this* place I thought it was a shit hole. It was dirty. It still kind of looks like Beirut. They don't finish the walls on anything, they don't paint half the stuff, the rebar is stick-ing out of everything. It's a third world place. Although often, when I'm on the edge of town and I look out at the mountains, that part looks beautiful. But the town itself has never struck me as very attractive."

I can't help but glance around at the house, to the carved *cantera* stone fireplace next to the sofa where Dave sits. Beyond, full-length white curtains shield the terrace from afternoon sun. Palms trees and the mature plantings of the garden below end in a tile-roofed *ramada* with a mirrored doorway in the back wall that makes the garden look like it goes on forever. The rooftop views reach further into the city. Sitting there I think of what sunset must be like every evening. Coming in, the long great room/dining room/kitchen with brick vaulted ceilings feel like endless hospitality. The hand-detailed wrought iron scroll-work of the railings invites your touch. I can see what Dave means. The place is a dump.

"I'm comparing it to other parts of the world," he goes on, gaining momentum. "It was one of the richest gold and silver mining countries, and you'd think with what they were building in Europe with that money some of it would have stayed here. But it was the differentness of it that appealed to me. It wasn't the U.S."

I ask whether that foreignness made it hard to settle in once they'd upended their lives in Virginia. "It wasn't hard at all," says Caren, ready with a rebuttal. "We fell right into it. There was never a time—except for problems with an architect—when we felt we made a mistake, or this is too hard. No, we were excited, we took it on as a challenge. It was fun; it was exploration with new eyes."

While this was going on their children had both finished school and were excited for them. One of them came down a couple years later and settled in San Miguel herself. Caren initially questioned the wisdom of this, but now admits to being totally wrong. "It's been a good fit for our daughter."

As time passed something began to gestate in Caren's mind. "When I tell this story it sounds weird to me. I just know this is true. Every single morning I woke and I thought, you feel really different. And then the second sentence was, you need to make a documentary film about this. I was half awake. Something was speaking to me, but in a not totally awake state. It went on for more than a year. I think it might have been two years." Although she was a painter, and had come at her therapist career through art, Caren had no experience in filmmaking.

"A bit of the film process," says Dave, "was to discover, what is it? Literally what is it that's making people be so crazy about this place." Unnecessarily, I remind them that the opening line of dialogue in Caren's film is, "Why am I here?"

"So it was two things," she continues, "trying to understand what happened to me, like the way I feel so different. And I wanted to know if I was alone. I really didn't know if these other people felt the same way. It's like any of us. We always think how we feel isn't the way anyone else feels. So it's a shock to do the thirty-nine interviews [in the film]. Three quarters of the people used the word home."

I point out that the word is capable of broad definition. Yet as I watched the film a number of times I began to feel it was more profound than I had initially thought. I also began to worry that there might be more overlap between our two projects than I wanted. Caren points out that one is a film and the other a book, and that there are intrinsic differences. One difference I point out is that while Caren is prominent in her film, I want my presence in this book to be small, mostly the guy wearing a staff tee shirt who sets up the equipment, asks a few questions, then turns out the lights and locks the door at the end.

"And that's what I wanted to do! That's why it took three and a half years."

"The film," says Dave, "started out totally opposite. She was not going to be in it."

"I had my heels in the sand. I was not going to be in it. I'm not narrating it. I'm a very stubborn woman."

As work went on it became clear that the project was missing something critical, but Caren had an extreme reluctance to step before the camera. "It was two things," she explains. "There are hardly any pictures of me, and there are a million pictures of Dave and the kids. I like to take the pictures, but more important, I was afraid of being judged. I was afraid people would say, 'Who does she think she is, making a film about herself?' I can tell you where it comes from; family stuff, where you're not supposed to be the center of attention."

But somehow Caren comes off as poised and relaxed, not professional in the sense that she'd appeared in other films, but natural, without any sense of awkwardness or shyness.

"It was like therapy to me," she says.

"In the original footage she was horrible," says Dave. "It was like somebody had given her drugs."

"Sometimes I would set the camera up in my studio alone." Eventually it came.

At this point I raise an issue I had been thinking

about for some time, ever since I knew I'd be talking to Dave and Caren. As I try to put these conversations in a condition to be read by intelligent humans, I keep bumping against the imperfect way people really speak. Clever, well educated, sensitive, and above all, articulate people, it turns out, can hardly put a sentence together or complete a rational thought as they talk. Myself included, but at least I know what I was trying to say. Every reporter has noticed this.

So I edit. I substitute words when they have said what they couldn't have meant. I drop the false starts. I eliminate the 'you knows' and all the similar filler words and phrases. And I sit there opposite the Crosses wondering about the same process writ large as they cut 120 hours of footage into fifty-three minutes of finished film. How could it make any sense? How could it resemble at all what people had said?

"I knew right away what was good," says Caren. "The cream rose to the top."

"But," I ask, "is the film true?" This is equivalent to asking if the three and a half years she spent on it was wasted. "Because it's been worked up and worked over and cut back and forth." My arms are making broad slashing motions. She probably thinks this is what I imagine film editing is like. It's done with a machete.

"I think it's absolutely honest. It's honest for me, so it's my truth."

"It's a little more difficult here," adds Dave, who has countless hours of his time in the project too. "You can do splices and cut stuff, but truth is hard. It was her truth at that time." There is a moment of silence while we're thinking about this. Truth has different meanings to each of us. The demand to get at it and portray it faithfully is clear; how to get access to it and identify it consistently when you do have it is not.

"You asked something twice," Caren says, "that I didn't answer. Did I have trouble leaving who I was before? That was the biggest struggle I had. My ego was so connected with 'I'm a therapist.' That's who I was for twenty-seven years. So I'm Dave's wife, I'm Jordan and Carly's mother, and I'm a therapist, that's who I am. And all of a sudden, I wasn't."

I've had hints of this before, but no one has stated it so bluntly. The high-powered lawyer or doctor comes down here and no one kowtows to him anymore. No one even asks him what he did in his work life. It's out of context. He wonders what his context now is, where grubby painters and eccentric writers seem to have more status than he does in this peculiar community.

"That was absolutely horrifying in a way—that's too strong a word," she adds.

Was being a painter part of this litany?

"I also thought I was a painter, but not being a therapist was really very important."

"Painting got co-opted," says Dave. "She was a painter, came back from Italy, got a job as an art therapist. And then her boss really liked what she was doing and said she should go back to grad school and become a therapist. She did, and left painting."

It makes me wonder whether Dave had similar identity issues.

"Not here. I did that. I took a trip; I thought I was Mr. Cool staying in Nice. All of a sudden I'm seeing myself through other people's eyes. I met people and they

183

would say, 'What do you do?' That's always everybody's first question--not here, but in other places. Are you a writer? You say, 'I'm not working.' 'Are you a painter?' No. Then they're scared because I'm like fifty. This guy doesn't have a job. He probably got laid off. It stops the conversation. I'd see that in their eyes and I'd think, who am I now? I'm not any of those things. That happened to me before, so when I came down here it was already over."

"And you dealt with it," adds Caren.

"But there are people who come down," says Dave, "who aren't ready to change. And they go back. It is really a significant move out of the culture you were in, and as Caren says in the film, you're not part of this culture and you're no longer part of *that* culture. After a while here—it takes a few years—but after a while here you see the United States in such a different way. Not only the political stuff, but the whole system.

"We were just in East Germany [on tour promoting the film at film festivals] and a guy was saying that the first time the wall came down and he could go to the other side he was stunned; he had to come back because he was overwhelmed. So much stuff, so many choices, so much of everything. I remember going back the first time after a few years to California. I walked into a supermarket and asked, 'Where's the water.' They said, aisle three. *All* of aisle three was water!

"Being here removes you from that enough so that you see it as just ridiculous. The amount of food wasted in two supermarkets in LA would feed everybody who's hungry in San Miguel. I find it hard to talk to a lot of people when I go back, because they're so driven, even if they look like they're not driven. We're not on the same plane any more."

So does Dave feel withdrawn there, mute?

"My last trip I was a month in LA in a little apartment in Santa Monica, the Venice Beach area, and I'd get up in the morning, ride my bike for an hour and a half, stop for a coffee or breakfast some place. I go rollerblading. I do my meditation, I go out to dinner, I don't talk to anybody for a month."

Does he miss the conversation? A month is a long time.

"I was happier than on any other trip there."

"He's a big talker," adds Caren. "He connects with people here, but there he has less connection."

In terms of penetrating Mexican culture and society, the experience of the Crosses is not much different from that of others. There are Mexicans they feel are their friends, but not close friends. They know everyone on their block, but don't see them socially. Dave points out that this is the same as on their block in Virginia Beach. "If someone had trouble," Dave says, "you'd help them out. But they weren't our close friends."

"That's interesting," adds Caren. "In the film I say I don't have close Mexican friends, but they influence me. People have attacked me for that. They think I don't speak Spanish because I said that, which isn't true. It's a closed society. Mexican women my age have six sisters. They're not looking for new friends." This is something I've come across here before. Virtually no one has said that their Mexican friends are in the first rank of their friends.

"I have two answers," says Caren. "There's a distrust of anybody outside. They really aren't interested in us like that. There was a Mexican friend of mine I offered to lend a copy of the film to when it was done. I said, 'Do you have a DVD player?' She said no. I said, 'Well, here's the DVD and you can borrow a player from a friend.' She said, 'I don't have any friends.' I was shocked. What do you say? I never heard anybody say they didn't have any friends.

"She has four sisters. She has four children and a husband. She has cousins. I've read about this phenomenon in books but I didn't really get it until somebody said to me, 'I don't have any friends.' It's not in their culture to go find a friend outside of their family."

This is more of an explanation than I'd gotten before.

On the other hand, the film has been highly praised and well received locally, in the States, and internationally. I ask if one of the resulting changes in her life is that Caren has made many more friends. Is that part of the changes in the five years since she shot it? Of course, but there is more. "I've grown up a lot. I've gained self-confidence. It's like I got undressed for this movie. It feels like a lot of my anxiety is gone."

I ask if she means that she put her innermost thoughts out there to be examined. "Right. I'm very different now. I'm more comfortable in my own skin."

"I'll give you one example," adds Dave. "As a therapist in Virginia she had a very good reputation, and she was asked by the local TV station to come on and do a presentation. And she was pumping Xanax to get calm enough to go in front of the camera."

"If I had to give a talk on anorexia in front of eighty people I'd be a wreck for a week. Now, it's 'Give me a chance!'"

"Now she comes out afterward high as a kite from interacting with everybody. It doesn't matter what the questions are."

"I realized that the film--we talked before about how you think you're alone, your feelings are just yours and you're a little crazy--well this film brings that out in people. They identify and afterwards they want to talk about it. So I think my therapist's personality wants to talk about it. I just want to hear, 'What did it bring up for you?'"

"People here," Dave says, "do use the film to have friends over. They show the film and then they have dinner and discuss it. It is really a lot about, 'What are you doing with your life?'"

I can't resist asking whether another film is shaping up in Caren's head.

"Yes. I've had one for about two and a half years." She doesn't want to say any more. People have suggested that these ideas can be exhausted by talking about them before they're fleshed out. She will only say that it's not a personal film and it does take place in San Miguel. And it's a documentary. "I know it will take about twenty years to make it.

"There's something I think is interesting that didn't go in the [first] film. It's about what happened in 2001. After September 11, in October, the real estate market had been flat for four years, and suddenly the real estate brokers' phones were ringing off the hook. People, when I told them that story, they think it's because people got scared. That's not what I think it was. It was about people saying, oh when I'm old I'll move to San Miguel, or oh, when we have enough money, or when...."

"And at that point the 'when' part got cut," I suggested.

"And the other interesting thing to me was that when Bush got reelected..."

"It was the biggest single boom in real estate here," cuts in Dave. "It doubled or tripled."

"You would see people in restaurants or the *jardin* who were saying, 'We've had it. We're looking for a house.'"

"What she was saying a while ago," adds Dave, "I think is true. In our eyes, it's very different from the way it was ten years ago and it's not such a big adventure anymore, because there are more restaurants and more people and it's easier to do everything and you can pay things by Internet. So that part of it has become more first-worldly. But I'm sure for someone coming from New York or Minneapolis or Hartford it's a huge adventure. Can you drink the water here, can you do this--all the stuff we don't even think about. I see more people here; the mix seems to be skewing more toward retirees. Fewer artists and writers."

I suggest that you can still have a good conversation here, and this has been one of them. Dave senses me moving toward wrapping this up, but he wants to talk about people who come here and then leave. "I think often it's because they don't get the kind of adulation they were used to getting in the States. It looks wonderful here and they have friends and then they aren't really anybody. They don't get to be anybody special. And so they go back."

"Or they become head of some charity," says Caren.

"No, but even that doesn't work."

"We're not in that group," says Caren, "so we can't address that."

I've heard a lot about the different social strata here. Are they part of any of them?

"We don't know any of them," says Caren.

I suggest they're cherry-picking the whole gringo group.

"We have some really great friends here and that's it," she adds.

Which sets up my perennial question, would anything make them go back? A long silence. "It would have to be one hellacious opportunity for something I really wanted to do," says Dave.

"I used to think that each house we lived in would be our house forever," adds Caren, "but now I'm mature enough to know that anything can happen. I'm not saying I'll be here forever, and I know that I could move back, and I'm not the same person, so it would be OK."

"It's hard to be a different person there, because the rest of the place isn't," says Dave.

"There's the peer pressure of, oh do I have the right shoes? That comes up."

And if they weren't here, where would they be?

"If I knew that, I'd probably be there," says Dave.

"We're exactly where we want to be," she adds.

Dave nods in agreement. "At the moment, this is it. It's just that I haven't found anyplace else that I want to be, and this is easy in the meantime."

Even though San Miguel has changed?

"Yes, but I don't like to talk about that," she says.

CHAPTER 15

YOU HAVEN'T MENTIONED THE SUNSETS

Few people I came across had been to San Miguel at an earlier age than Linton Pitluga. He arrived at fifteen with his family while his father, a college science teacher from the State University of New York in Oswego, took a sabbatical and studied painting. Linton enjoyed the nearly year-long visit and made friends among the American kids. He and Phyllis were back for a week in the 1970s, but never thought about living here. Forty-six years after his first visit he changed his mind. He's not impulsive.

By that time his two sisters both owned houses here, and he and Phyllis were shopping for a retirement location less chilly than Chicago. They looked at the South Pacific and the Caribbean, found the beaches and the scuba diving attractive, but thought the islands in both areas lacked cultural and social activities to keep them busy. Neither was looking for a sedentary retirement. "Stir crazy," is the term that comes to Linton's mind when he thinks of sitting on the beach and watching the waves roll in.

Phyllis had recently retired as chief astronomer at the Adler Planetarium in Chicago and had traveled extensively in Latin America. In addition to numerous Mexico trips for vacations, she had been summoned to Peru in the early eighties to assist with investigating the Nasca Lines, the enormous ancient drawings on the Peruvian plains that have puzzled both visitors and residents for generations, since they can be seen completely only from the air. She spent about four years out of the next ten in the field, measuring, mapping, and theorizing. She subsequently determined both the purpose of the lines and their age, and developed a hypothesis that demonstrated how they could have been drawn with the tools available to the ancients and without the assistance of space aliens, as others have suggested.

Although she published a scientific paper on the subject earlier, she is currently at work on a mass-market book that promises to be the definitive popular book on the subject. When not at her word processor, she water skis whenever she can. Inevitably this requires leaving San Miguel. She and Linton are thinking of docking a boat at a lake in Texas.

Meanwhile they live high on the edge of a walled townhouse development on the eastern side of town overlooking the Querétaro Road. Their views appear to stretch for 20 miles. They rearranged the house plan from the original so that the living, dining, and kitchen areas are on the upper floor, to catch the views. The bedrooms are now on the lower level.

"You don't need the view when your eyes are closed," says Linton.

He has a cordial, low-key manner that may be part of being in San Miguel for the last four years, but I suspect it was in place long before and is simply an excellent fit for the town. Phyllis is more matter of fact, clearly looking at things from a scientist's point of view. Retirement for her means sleeping late, but the rest of her life seems active and even busy, especially with her book now in the works.

The catalyst for their decision to move here was a visit to one of Linton's sisters. Out by themselves, they wandered into a realty office. Before that they had looked at California, Florida, Texas, as well as other areas in the U.S. "We had been looking at a lot of places," says Phyllis, "but we hadn't found the right place, and I would say that when we were walking around on our own here in San Miguel, it just seemed right. With both his sisters having houses here, it seemed like the right thing to do. That was the second biggest reason for me, after climate."

"A strong part of it," continues Linton, "is the atmosphere and the fact that there are lots of interesting people here and lots of interesting things going on."

Phyllis didn't realize this at first. "That became more of a surprise for me after making the commitment."

I wonder aloud whether they would have found the same thing in the Caribbean.

"I think if the Caribbean had more of the pyramids, or that kind of culture, but it's really pretty spartan in that sort of history," she says. "It's really just the beach and boating and being in a warm tropical climate."

"There's another factor," adds Linton. "I like the fact that this is a city rather than a little town. Because of that it has a lot of things to offer, restaurants, lectures and so on."

"That came as a big surprise to me," Phyllis says, "how intellectually rich it is. I'm not an artsy person per se."

When the decision had been made there were no serious obstacles to moving. It helped that Linton's sisters were already established in town, and another family that Linton had known from his early visit was still here.

Once established Linton taught English to Mexican kids and Phyllis did mentoring to a young archaeology student and organized eclipse programs at the Botanical Gardens. She also writes the monthly astronomy column in *Atencion*, the English language paper. The Nazca Lines book makes heavy demands on her schedule, but she still squeezes in the occasional golf game.

They have one Mexican friend, a man with a telescope and an interest in astronomy. He is married to an American woman. They would like to have more. "That has been one of the disappointments. We had been thinking of joining Malanquin [the local private golf club with many Mexican members], and we've actually had a few other opportunities that one would have thought in the U.S. environment would have blossomed into an invitation. But we never got the reciprocal invitation."

The presence of so much poverty makes them conscious of how they display jewelry. Phyllis points to a fine piece from New Mexico that she says she would never wear on the street. "I try not to be ostentatious when I'm out and about. Of course, we've seen the poverty before, certainly in Los Angeles and Chicago, and I've never thought of myself as wealthy, although I'm sure that by their standards we are. Of course I encountered this down in Peru too. People thought I must live like a television starlet."

"When I lived here the first time," adds Linton, "San Miguel was a lot poorer. It seems like the middle class has expanded quite dramatically over the interim, but in riding I would go out to some of these little pueblos, and it was an education to see people living in houses that were pretty primitive. They probably didn't have running water, probably had an outhouse. Pigs, chickens, kids were running in and out. It always gave me a more realistic sense of what real life was like, and that we were living in, not a make believe world, but a world that was different in the States. Also it helped me to think about what was important. The Mexicans manage to still be pretty happy people, even though life isn't perfect."

When Phyllis sees people on the street with their hands out it makes her think of how hard she's worked, and it reminds her of all the begging she saw at Union Station in Chicago going to and from work.

While being here does not connect them much to an earlier part of their lives, Linton is occasionally sparked by something he sees and thrust back to his first visit in the late fifties. Phyllis sees constant reminders of the Spanish style architecture of the Los Angeles she grew up in. Neither of them sees any reason to go back to the States other than a possible medical one.

"One of the things I might enjoy doing is some house swapping and living some other places," says Phyllis. "I like immersing myself in different cultures. But that's not leaving here. This feels like home. As long as Mexico is stable, there's no reason not to be here. There are more murders going on in Chicago right now than in all of Mexico."

What Mexico offers that is most important to Phyllis is the climate, while Linton feels it's just a good experience to be living somewhere else. "Folks are friendly here," he continues. "They make it easy for you to live here, in most respects. If you're a little bit laid back you can get by pretty well with the situation. We have a neighbor who is Cuban, and he knows a lot of Mexicans. He was telling me that he doesn't hear negative things about the U.S. and Americans."

The existence of the Internet, cable TV, inexpensive international phone services, mail drops that facilitate bringing packages and letters quickly and reliably across the border diminish the very sense of a border. It is possible to be as closely or as loosely connected as anyone would wish. Because San Miguel is a popular destination, it's possible to remain close to friends. Seeing them for a week at a time often results in seeing more of them than just occasional dinners in the States.

Linton recalls that his parents didn't seem to miss these closer ties. They didn't complain about the lack of a telephone. There was at that time one bank with ties to the U.S. that transferred and changed money.

But the diet was different. "When we lived here [in 1959], you ate Mexican. You couldn't get Campbell's soup. The beef was just horrible. The butcher shops didn't have refrigeration, so they would have a carcass hanging there that was black, covered with flies."

From the roof garden, where the views go on for nearly 360 degrees, pots of herbs supply Linton's cooking projects, at which he is expert. He finds the beef is much improved. The barbecue itself, however, resembles something from the early history of railroading. It's too complicated, says Linton, and the local newspaper doesn't have the right composition for lighting the charcoal properly.

Neither of them finds the tourists objectionable,

although they don't seem overly friendly. After living in Chicago for years, they don't expect to recognize people on the street. "I get the feeling from some American residents here that they disdain tourists," says Linton. "Somehow they feel superior."

The Pitlugas stay in touch with news from the States using both cable TV and the Internet. Although they did not support President Bush on most issues, and have higher hopes for Obama, they do approve of Bush's treatment of Mexico.

In the end, for Phyllis, the special flavor of Mexico can be summed up in one word. "What I love here are the fiestas. I think they're great. They're happening almost monthly. I love them because they're native; it's not like the Easter parade kind of thing. It's real, it has a deep core to it."

"I just like Mexicans," says Linton. "They're just nice people, nice to be with, a good sense of humor."

But they both agree that it may not be for everyone. Red tape can be a frustrating concern, especially in trying to build a home here. "You need to be either ready for it or willing to do it," says Phyllis, "and then you're OK. If you're not, you're going to be bad mouthing the place. But I find it a comfortable home, to sum it up."

"You haven't mentioned the sunsets," adds Linton.

❈❈❈

When I finished writing up this initial conversation, I was left with the feeling of two experienced Latin America hands settling back into an environment they knew well. Coming to San Miguel had involved no special surprises, no great tribulations or sacrifices. Looking out their windows, they saw little they hadn't seen before. What the story lacked in drama it supplied in smoothness, something that can be in short supply here for newcomers. There was a kind of unaffected confidence to it that suggested, yes, it happens this way too.

There were no parallels to their story in my own experience or in that of others I've been talking to. It was almost as if they had done it by the book, a book none of the rest of us had been able to find. That's why when the catastrophe struck it was all the more shocking, but then, it had nothing to do with Mexico.

Just a few days after we talked Phyllis and Linton were driving up to northern Illinois to prepare for the sale of a condo they owned on Fox Lake. In Missouri a truck changed lanes blindly and forced them off the freeway into the median. Their Nissan SUV rolled over several times. Phyllis was driving. Her left arm was crushed and a vertebra in her neck cracked. Linton was thrown from the car when his seat belt failed. He thinks he went through the sunroof. Although he broke no bones, there were deep cuts all over his body. They were taken to different hospitals, and it was five hours before Linton would even know that Phyllis had survived. For some time she had to wear a "halo," a device that keeps her neck from moving while the bone fuses. Months of this was accompanied by reconstructive surgery on her arm.

It was six months before they could return home to Mexico. Did this life changing experience change their view of San Miguel? Not at all. Phyllis is getting ready to take up golf again. Linton is tinkering with his barbecue. They're just glad to be home.

CHAPTER 16

DECONSTRUCTING DALLAS

The Guadiana neighborhood lies east of Ancha de San Antonio, a wide commercial street winding south from centro, which becomes the highway to Celaya. Guadiana is more or less flat until, on its opposite edge, it ramps up toward Prolongacion Aldama, its eastern limit. Within its borders the streets are narrow and quiet. There are few shops other than a good bakery and a single hair salon, tucked into a space that must have begun as a garage. There is no thoroughfare, and because of this, most people who find themselves driving within Guadiana are either leaving or on their way home.

Some are already home.

Laurie and Lisa, a couple in their early 40s from Dallas, have no car. They are living, for the moment, in a tiny *casita* with a bedroom, sitting room, kitchenette and bath. It adjoins what will be their house, two stories of neocolonial stone and stucco now mostly fleshed out, awaiting finishes. Surrounding the central court, which will ultimately have a pool, are graceful gray *cantera* stone arches on both floors. Through the back wall an opening overlooks a garden space in the side yard that will include a small amphitheater. As Laurie describes it, "It is an oval,

198

three tier theater in the round. We designed it for the production of outdoor theater, performance art, or musical events."

I had walked past this construction project before, thinking it a day spa or upscale bed and breakfast. I'd never known the owners' names, and as I now find myself ringing the bell of the casita, I don't realize at first that it's part of the larger building.

The door is opened by a tall slender blonde with short hair. Wearing jeans and a gray tee shirt that reads, "Kiss my Grits," she introduces herself as Lisa. Laurie is immediately behind her. Shorter, engaging, with dark hair with a single streak of gray, her jeans are topped by a navy tee shirt.

We arrange ourselves in the small sitting room, and Lisa begins the story of how they came to San Miguel. Not surprisingly, it has a political component. "We decided to move to Mexico on the day after the election of 2004, when George Bush was reelected. We did not know much about it; we had only been to beach towns and border towns, and we just wanted a change of direction, a change of environment. We talked to friends in Dallas, and we had a very good friend who had lived in Mexico for some time. She was our Spanish teacher, and she recommended that we try San Miguel. She said, 'Don't quit your jobs tomorrow, but go there and see what you think.' We came down here in December of 2004 for three weeks and totally fell in love. We didn't want to leave."

What was it about Mexico? Why not England or Senegal?

"She," says Lisa, pointing at Laurie, "has always been really attracted to Mexico."

"Even though I didn't know central Mexico," Laurie adds, "the Mexican artists and the culture and the Mexican people in the States have always had..."

Lisa jumps in, "We had some good relationships with people in Dallas who are Mexicans who have emigrated to Texas. We love them, their culture, their spirit, their colors, their *joie de vivre*; we love everything about that. Maybe France would be great too, but we didn't want to be that far. We liked the idea of warmer weather, rather than cold weather like Canada."

"It took us fourteen months," says Laurie, "to save enough money, and sell two houses, and I was finishing a degree."

"We moved here in March of 2006."

Laurie had been an artist for some time and was finishing her Ph.D. in esthetics. On the wall next to her is a vertical example of her work. On a blue background of varying intensity, three red figures divide the space, themselves punctuated by yellow. Two smaller red figures and a red circle dance around them. Hints of warm green surface, mostly to pop the other colors. It is measured, rhythmic. It appears to be about the relationship of primary colors and motion. I'm sure Laurie would have a different take.

"I had finished all my coursework right before we moved and then spent the first year and a half writing the dissertation, so I've had my Ph.D. now for a year." As a painter myself I ask whether the advanced degree was a kind of validation, something she felt she needed beyond the basic ability to put brushes to canvas in a way that worked. Or was she delving into the process of painting on an intellectual level as a compliment to what her hands and eyes could do?

"It wasn't about credentials," she says, shaking her head. "Because I paint, I do digital video and digital photography, and conceptual sculpture. I really did it because I was painting or doing other forms of art ten hours a day, and Lisa, being a lawyer, worked a lot. I was alone in my studio, and I needed interaction and inspiration. So I went more for the ideas. It was a really cool Ph.D. program: half studio art and half theory. The only time I've been back to Dallas for any length of time is when I went back to do my oral defense for my degree. Other than that, I don't go back."

Laurie already had her master's degree in education, and in an earlier career she'd been a counselor and therapist, and had run a restaurant as well. What they found in the fourteen months of dismantling their lives in Dallas was how enmeshed they were. Lisa did not work for a law firm, but in the legal department of a large company. "I had a really good job, and so deciding to quit that job was a real moment. I was deputy general counsel in the legal department. It was a big company, a $10 billion company. That was the hardest part for me, the decision to quit practicing law."

Lisa was then thirty-nine years old. Did people think she was nuts? "They may have, but they didn't say so. Most of the reactions I got were like, 'How cool!' The company I worked for had started out very small, and many people who started out with it made a lot of money along the way because the stock went up so much. A lot of people had left and done different things. Nobody was all that shocked."

But there must be fallout from this. Has Lisa ever

regretted all the money she could be making? Are there feelings of guilt? Does she sleep well? "No, not guilt. I would never say I feel guilty, but I can't say it hasn't crossed my mind. The person that we hired to replace me has now gotten the job I would love to have had. That I would have had if I had stayed. That was a little painful. But I don't feel any regret. I'm just so happy with my decision."

This must have required a shift in values. "My core values are the same, but as far as my daily values, where you just get in that rat race and you think things are so important, they aren't that important. All that translates into money, which is your scorecard at work. Once I got away from that, once I even made the decision to get away from it during the last year I was there, my whole system of what matters in life changed. I find when I talk to my friends back in the States I want to say things to them that are so stupid that if someone said them to me a few years ago I wouldn't have listened. I was *in* it; I was busy. I was climbing the corporate ladder and doin' what you do. Now I think, God, I don't see how people do it. I would hate to have to go back."

But while no one from her company has come down to see first hand what Lisa has done with her life, two of Laurie's professors have. Because she was a student, it was less difficult for her to disentangle the threads of her life. "It was because I didn't have this fantastic job. It was easy for me emotionally because I was so ready. My dissertation was basically autobiographical and explored the social and political environment of the United States over the past five years. My last show was called *Being Moved*, like being moved internally to move from the country."

Does this mean that the move was more about what Mexico wasn't? Was it an escape? "I think, in the beginning," says Lisa, "when we decided to leave the States, it *was* more about leaving. But once we had spent some time here and gotten to know San Miguel, it was more about being completely and fanatically in love with San Miguel. And now that we've been here two and a half years you just couldn't drag us out of here."

I suggest that in spite of this there must have been some difficult times settling in.

"You know," says Lisa, shaking her head with a wry smile, "there have hardly been any hard parts."

My response is that this makes for a boring interview. I want chaos, agony, tears.

"We bought our house," responds Laurie, "not this house that we're building, but the house we're getting ready to sell, over the Internet, sight unseen. Every time our realtor would say she had a house in our price range, so come and see it, it was gone."

Finally, on the realtor's assurance that this house was perfect, they purchased it without coming to San Miguel. The house was perfect, except that it lacked a yard for their three dogs. "We're building this house for the dogs," says Laurie with a laugh.

San Miguel is an easy place to make friends, and although I keep hearing about all the strata here that don't mix, (the 'Gangs of San Miguel' theory) no one professes to be part of one.

"We have friends," adds Laurie, "in every age group, every interest, gay, straight, whatever. The diversity of our truly good friends, not just acquaintances, is absolutely delightful."

"I spent the first year that we lived here volunteering as a teacher at the *Biblioteca*," says Lisa. "That was really fun, but then they sent me on the adult program. We're not into just one thing."

At this point Laurie would be doing a lot of painting if her studio were ready. The company Lisa formerly worked for has hired her three times to work on big projects. She has written their last two annual reports and a sustainability report.

Laurie and Lisa also were involved in the concept phase of setting up a Tex Mex bar, which occupied them for nearly a year. But they have not fallen into the pitfall of replicating their level of busyness in the States. "I can see that it would be easy," says Lisa. "But the idea of sitting around in a hammock all day, well that's just not who we are, either. We feel busy, but it's not the kind of busy that it was in the States."

"And we get to be together all day," adds Laurie. "In the States I entertained myself and went to school and did my art and she went to work. It's fun because we love to hang out together."

"And we have more close friends here than we had in the States. There were people we were sorry to leave, but [there's a greater] volume of people we get to spend a lot of time with here, because we have time and they have time. There's some common denominator in people that will do what we've all done, moving to a foreign country, which is a great thing to do. There's a lot of interesting people here."

"We just had an interesting experience. When we moved here we decided to get health insurance that would cover us here or in the U.S."

"Because we were terrified of the health care system here," adds Lisa. "That was our one fear. If we ever get sick we're going back to the States."

"We were in a position one month ago where Lisa had to have back surgery, immediately. We found a doctor in Querétaro [thirty miles away], a neurosurgeon who is unbelievable."

"I had a ruptured disk, which had moved."

"The personalization of the health care, the knowledge; it was a beautiful experience. Just four weeks ago she had surgery in Querétaro. We found a doctor who was trained at the University of Michigan, and we loved him."

"And our internist we love, and our dentist."

"To have your neurosurgeon's cell phone number and have him answer when you call. I would trust the doctors here that I've worked with to tell me if I should go back to the States."

Laurie is still thinking about whether they came for what Mexico was, or were they fleeing something. I suggest, quoting someone I once heard, that you're here either because you're wanted or because you're not wanted. Both feel they were wanted in Dallas. "We really loved our lifestyle in Dallas," she says. "We had the best friends in the world. I loved school and my art career was good and Lisa loved her job. We had fun. We've been together almost twelve years now, and we've always had fun since we've been together. It wasn't like life sucked then and now it's good. We were just ready for a change of the political and social climate."

"The change of pace was a bonus," adds Lisa. "We didn't realize how fast we were living until we stopped doing that. And here, hardly ever does anyone ask what do you do or what did you do."

But to the extent that people's identities are based on what they do or did for a living, there can be a loss of identity in settling here. Some don't miss it. Others may find a loss of status in it. I think it comes inevitably with retirement, and isn't only associated with San Miguel. Sometimes for couples this also means an adjustment in their relationship. Tasks and responsibilities get redistributed.

Lisa and Laurie have not found any substantive change in their relationship. The main difference is that here they can spend much more time together. With Laurie there is an unstated assumption that she will continue with her art projects, but for Lisa there's a substantial break with her prior identity. I usually think that lawyers are lawyers about twenty-three hours a day, but I see in Lisa no sense of drift or confusion. She just seems happy.

But there is a downside. This place has its drawbacks as much as any other. Sometimes it's also what you leave behind. "We miss our friends," says Lisa. "We spent a lot of time with them on the weekends. It's a tradeoff. But I personally never expected we would have so many friends here. It was so hard to leave our friends and come here and know no one."

Working on setting up the Tex Mex bar gave them an opportunity to meet a number of Mexicans and their families, and that gave them a sense of penetrating Mexican culture. They have two friends they would consider in their first tier of friends, but, as they point out, they speak English. Yet they feel privileged. "To have the honor of getting to know Mexicans and to really understand their culture, even though we were drawn to this culture before we came here, it's even more beautiful than we thought."

"The Mexican people," adds Laurie, "and I know you can't generalize, are deeply kind, deeply human."

"Like when I had my back surgery everyone was nice and supportive, but our Mexican friends were ringing the doorbell. They don't call first, they come and bring something, they send something. They're just such great people; they're loving, they're caring. They will do anything for you in a time of need."

The two women are divided about how closely to follow events in the States. Lisa watches the news every day; Laurie relies on Lisa's reports when she wants to know something specific, not much otherwise. "I have so many feelings about things," she says. "I spent a lot of time and trouble to get out of that environment, and I don't want to live in it via computer or telephone and TV."

"But I stay in touch," says Lisa, "because I think I might be called for another job from the States and I want to be totally informed."

Laurie feels that her best response is through her art. "I devoted the last five years that I lived in the States to speaking to what I found upsetting."

I ask if she considers her art political. "Yes, but you wouldn't necessarily know that by looking at it. My art is very philosophically, socially, politically, rooted in humanity, which is all aspects of the individual and the environment, whether it be social or political."

I feel like part of this got past me, but I've never had much of a theoretical take on art. "My art," she continues, "is not a political message, my art is an expression

207

of my humanity in this day and age. It's so personal what I'm expressing, so it's emotional, social, political, environmental -- all of those things."

"And some people may not even get it that you're making a statement," adds Lisa.

I ask if they are different from other Americans who live here, wondering at the same time if I should stop asking this. Everyone has been different in each one of these conversations. Maybe I should ask how they are the same.

"I do feel that we're different than everyone else who lives here," says Lisa. "But I don't think that's anything new. We're weird and always have been, no matter where we live."

Has San Miguel changed since they first toured here in 2004?

"There's either more focus on the violence around Mexico, or there is more violence in Mexico, which I feel has had some impact here."

"I don't think there's been any increase in violence in San Miguel," adds Laurie.

"We may be idiots, but we don't feel afraid, any more afraid than we did in Dallas."

"Oh, I feel much less afraid than I did in Dallas," says Laurie. "Just walking down the street my level of centeredness versus mild anxiety about potential threats is much better. The way strangers deal with the male/female thing here is much more comfortable."

But what doesn't work? They seem to have come to earth here in a fundamental way.

"The only thing that would make us go back is money," says Lisa. "If we ran out of money we would try everything. You'd have to shoot us and take our bodies back."

As for where else they might settle if not Mexico, they would go further south, to another Spanish speaking country. While they aren't fully comfortable with Mexican politics, they don't think things are much different in the rest of Latin America.

Are they at all connected to the gay and lesbian community?

"I don't think there is one," says Lisa. "To our minds there's nothing organized about it. Half the time we don't even know someone is gay until we've known him for a little while. People are who they are, and you're the same wherever you go. We have friends who have moved here and been extremely disappointed, because they thought it was going to change who they are. And it doesn't. We were extremely happy in Dallas, and we're extremely happy here. The people that we know here that we like to hang out with are all happy people and were happy people before they got here. When you come to a city and you expect it to change who you are, it's not going to happen."

"What Lisa is trying to say is that if you're bitter and unhappy you can do that here too."

"You can change your circumstances," says Lisa. "If you have a job that makes you unhappy or if you're unhappy with your drive to work, you can change that, but you can't change how you perceive what goes on around you. The people who move here and complain about everything, how slow things are and how *mañana* is never *mañana*, are people who are not adjusting well to this community. The reason they don't is that they weren't happy

209

with what they were, and they brought it with them."

The current house project, months overdue, is an example. They don't complain, nor do they know when it will be finished. They have been living for months in this small casita while their first house is being readied to put on the market. You take Mexico on its own terms.

"We literally walk outside," says Lisa, "and we look around at the people, we look up at the churches, we look at the buildings. We just go, 'Oh my God I can't believe we live here,' and it is just so beautiful. We love the energy of this town."

"The values, the way the parents treat the children," adds Laurie, "and adults treat each other. I keep using the words 'so deeply humane.' I know that's not very articulate, but there's a kindness and a respect for individual life that's here on a daily basis. People don't really care whether you're gay or straight or agnostic or atheist."

"They care about how you treat them. It works for us very well."

CHAPTER 17

SAN MIGUEL WAS THE ONE I HATED

Although San Miguel de Allende was a logical alternative to retiring in a trailer park in Keokuk, Iowa, it wasn't Marcia Loy's first choice in Mexico. Starting to think about retirement in 2000, when the stock market was retreating and so was her money, it was her daughter who originally brought up the idea. Its initial appeal was that it might work better for a person on limited retirement funds.

At that point Marcia had seen Mexico City, Juarez, Taxco and Cuernavaca. The beach communities held no appeal for her. She did not care for humidity and was not fond of the feeling of sand between her toes. In 2002 she returned with her daughter and looked at Guadalajara, Chapala, and Ajijic. At that point she thought Ajijic, a community on the north shore of Lake Chapala with a large population of Canadian and U.S. retirees, had the most potential.

"Then in 2004 we came to three cities, and I liked one, loved one, and I hated one. I went to Morelia, San Miguel, and Guanajuato. San Miguel was the one I hated."

She says this ironically now, after being here more

than three years. Initially her reaction came partly from the Americans she saw, shouting in English as a way to make themselves understood to people who only spoke Spanish. "I wanted to put a paper bag over my head," she says. "Compared to Guanajuato, the one I loved, San Miguel seemed a little shabby, a little run down, most things in need of painting."

She decided to move to Guanajuato, the state capital and a college town, about sixty miles from San Miguel and closer to the Leon international airport. But the Cervantino Festival was underway in Guanajuato at that time and lodging was difficult to come by. She decided to settle in San Miguel for six months or so, then return to Guanajuato and settle in. "I told my daughter I knew what was going to happen. I'll meet people, make friends, find things to do, and I'm never going to move."

She was right.

Now she rents in an old house with an orange and dark red facade immediately next to the English library on Insurgentes. It's hard to tell how old it might be, these facades don't vary much, but it's in the oldest part of town. Outside the street throbs with buses and cars, and the foot traffic is constant to and from the Plaza Civica, just up the street another block. Today, two long rows of booths are set up to sell handmade toys crafted by the country people. Inside Marcia's building, beyond a small inner court, her apartment is on the second floor away from the noise.

You come in to a great room filled with low bookshelves and a fireplace. On the left wall is a large abstract painting whose mellow colors enhance the sense of calm and relaxation. Marcia Loy is a person who cares deeply about books and ideas. She writes the book column in *Atencion*, the local bilingual paper, and volunteers at the library. She is serious about writing herself and has two book projects in the works. These are both novels, the narrative dialogue-driven and reflective of the good-natured humor that also punctuates her own conversation.

Loy has not gone native. Her hair and clothes would put her right at home walking down Michigan Avenue in her home town, Chicago. Her grayish hair is cropped short and stylish: she has solved the problem some American women have in San Miguel, that of getting a hairdresser who's as good as the one back home.

After a year here she returned for a visit to Guanajuato, where she found it much too hectic. "You don't realize what a lovely pace of life we have here until you go somewhere else."

But in relocating to Mexico Marcia encountered the usual logistical problems. There was a house to prepare and sell, a lifetime accumulation of furniture to get rid of. It was a scary thing, she says. She liked Mexico, liked the people, but still, you don't know until you settle in whether you're going to continue liking it. She had also left the States earlier than she originally thought, without a lot of money.

"I had all these fantasies about what it would be like, but it was better. I was here maybe three months when I realized it had exceeded my wildest fantasies about how great it would be. I had lived in Evanston, Illinois for about twenty-five years, and after I'd lived there fifteen I would go to the grocery store and run into people I knew or have lunch in a restaurant and run into other people. I was here two years, and I couldn't even walk down the street without running into half a dozen people I knew. It's just a really great place to meet people and make friends and find things to do."

Marcia is not one to avoid thinking about her motives or reasons for relocating to another country as a single person at retirement age. For her, it was not because of any negative feelings about her situation or about the U.S. "I'm really glad I came here because I love the Mexican culture's emphasis on living today. It's something I don't think we do in the States. It's always about when I graduate from school, when I get a job, when I get a house, when I get married, when I have a baby, when we get a bigger house and a second car, and we just wait all of our lives until that magic time when we're going to be *happy.* Of course, it never happens because there's always something else you want. Here they have a sense of the fragility of life. Today's the day to be happy. I think I took to that right away.

"I used to get up at four o'clock in the morning when I worked [as a legal secretary], write in my journal, work out, do my meditation, and then I would hop on the train at 7:20, come back home at 6:30, eat dinner and go to bed."

Within two weeks of moving to Mexico she had relaxed into a place within herself that she didn't know existed. The sense of "get out of my way, I've got to make the train," has disappeared from her driving. She was aware of how the absolute *pace* of things pervaded everything she did in the States. Everyone she knew was the same way. There seemed to be no reason to question it.

"It was the idea that you're doing a lot, accomplishing a lot," she says, looking off over the rooftops as if at a different time and place, difficult now to recover. "Life is short and you have to do everything today." She shakes her head slowly. What an idea! The jumble of parapets, gardens, water tanks and flowers gives way to a view of the upper part of the *Parroquia*, the local cathedral. Bells begin to ring from a church far off. On the patio wall behind her ceramic lizards climb toward the sky. It was no surprise that this concept of life as a perpetual task list was among the first things to fall away after she settled in San Miguel.

But of course, it is the constant difference in the detail of everything that adds up to the overall strangeness of living somewhere else. "For the first two weeks I didn't leave the apartment. I didn't understand the money. I could make myself understood, but I didn't understand the responses. They talked too fast. I just stayed home and read."

Now her Spanish is liquid, if not fluent, and she is immersed in the English library, the Authors' Sala, two writers' and one readers' group. She finds there are distinct segments within the expatriate community, estimated at from five to seven thousand full time residents. "There is the cocktail set, the wealthy set, the volunteer types, the artistic types." They tend not to mingle much. It is possible, but more difficult to make friends with Mexicans. More difficult than she first thought. It is partly that the country is more formal in its manners than most Americans realize. Mexicans also entertain differently. Usually entire families are included. Americans tend to entertain without their children if it's not a holiday or family occasion. The Americans in San Miguel are generally, but not always, without children anyway.

Over time the question of identity emerges. Is a person different for having lived abroad for three and a half years? Does it depend on whether she has kept a residence in the States?

Marcia Loy acknowledges that she's given this some thought. Part of it is expressed by how closely she stays "in touch."

"I have a television set, but I don't have many channels. I don't have cable. There's one channel that's in Spanish, and it seems like they show mostly cartoons. I haven't missed being part of the news. I really like taking a vacation from that because it makes you crazy. I did go back two years ago and spent Christmas in the States. I was just astounded by all the advertising on television. I belong to the Fran Liebowitz school of thought on the news: what do they expect me to do about it? If you can't do anything about it and it's making you upset, because there's hardly ever any good news, then I don't understand this idea that somehow you have to be informed. I'm much more interested at this point in my life in my philosophical and spiritual development as a person than I am in what is going on in some other part of the world, including the U.S."

Nor does she much interest herself in local news and politics, partly because she feels she's a guest and it may not be appropriate for Americans to try to involve themselves in local affairs. She studied Latin American history in college and is up to speed on national politics, both current and going back as far as the war with the U.S. in 1846-8. Being from Chicago, she is not a political idealist, nor is she naive about how governments act. She feels that the governments of both countries are fully prepared to lie to their citizens. It's just politics, and does not deserve to be taken seriously. But barring a serious change in Mexican national politics, one that would create a hostile environment for Americans, she does not see herself as ever moving back to the States. "Think of what I would have to give up!" she says, seeing a return to the richest country in the world as a kind of privation, a narrowing of resources, a darkening of her future.

But for Marcia the most important reason for being here is not economic, it's cultural. "I liked living in Chicago, don't get me wrong, I lived there for thirty years. I went there from Miami so I'd have real weather." Eventually all the climate related issues she found in the Midwest became tiresome, shoveling the snow, cleaning out the rain gutters twice a year. There's not much she misses about it, except perhaps early spring, when she could sense from the way the air feels that winter has given up.

Marcia also misses supermarket and drugstore sales, where she could get tuna for 31 cents a can and stock up. She does without fat free sour cream and hot pastrami sandwiches. Low fat cheeses and ersatz mayonnaise made with soy. Vitamins on sale two for one. Aside from these minor things she does not feel she has sacrificed anything to live in Mexico. "Anything you give up you get back in a different way."

When I bring up the issue of how she might be different from other Americans who live here, she pauses for a while. "I have a group of friends who find customer service in Mexico to be abominable. I have had quite the opposite experience, but I also believe that what you expect is what you get. If you think that the plumber or the auto mechanic is going to cheat you, you'll find one who does. I'm fairly relaxed about things that happen. When my passport and FM3 [Mexico Resident Visa] were stolen in Argentina, I didn't get all bent out of shape. I mean, that must happen every day, all over the world."

Many of the Americans who live in San Miguel are here, she believes, because they can have a big fancy place for less money. "I didn't come here for that reason. It's more expensive than I expected it to be. Of course, San Miguel is more expensive than most places [in Mexico], and I'm not sure I would always stay here. But I didn't come here for that. I came here to enjoy the weather, enjoy the culture, and I love traveling around the country. I think it's like England: you could travel the rest of your life and not see the entire country.

"There's a warmth here that I don't think you find in...well, maybe in small towns [in the U.S.], but then you've got all the disadvantages of small towns, where people know everything that happened in your whole life. [The social life] is the best part about Mexico, or at least about this town. In Chicago I found, when I got divorced when I was forty-five, that I just felt I was invisible. With my married friends that I'd known for years, I was out, and it wasn't that they were inviting *him*, it was just that I was out. I had to make new friends. I discovered when I was riding on the el or the train to work that younger people looked right through me. I was invisible; I suddenly didn't count any more because I was forty-five. I hadn't expected that.

"Later, of course, it became a freeing concept that I was invisible, no one was paying attention. It wasn't like high school where they were all watching you, and I could just do anything I wanted."

San Miguel presents a different social structure, where Marcia has both married and single friends who invite her to parties and other social affairs. In addition, the younger Mexicans take the view that older people have knowledge and experience that they don't. They're not written off as irrelevant. "Young people in the States have completely forgotten this. I love being a single person here."

But is it safe? As much so as Ottumwa, Iowa or Paducah, Kentucky, she says. "A woman dropped me off here one day, in the middle of the day, and when I started to get out of her car she said, 'Have you got your keys out?' There were a hundred people within sight of me. Why would you say, hurry up and get in your house?"

The changes she has seen since she arrived three years ago include many more Americans coming here to flip houses, but on the plus side there are the new Mega and Liverpool stores, the Office Depot. The impending Walmart subsidiary may be less welcome to some. On balance, she sees most changes as positive.

Americans visiting as tourists can be both wonderful and terrible. "Some of the tourists that come here are lovely and really appreciate the culture, but some are just rude. A friend of mine had a person visit him who went up to the local corner store to get cream for his coffee, and he came back really angry. He said, 'These people don't even try to speak English.' That kind of attitude is really ugly. There's a guy that pounds on the library door at 10:01 every morning, and then when they finally open the door at 10:05, or whenever they are ready, he says, 'Oh, you guys finally woke up.'"

Marcia has gone back to the States just once, for

three weeks. She found it fun to go shopping, something she never enjoyed much when she lived there. "But the strangest thing to me was that in the background when you'd go to grocery stores or shopping centers, no one was speaking Spanish." She would love to go back to Chicago--which she did not visit on her single return to the States--but she has no immediate plans to do so. Somehow it's not a priority.

As she looks at changes in herself since her arrival, she immediately thinks of the ability to reinvent herself, to become someone she had always wanted to be, or didn't know she wanted to be, because she never had the time to think about it. "When I got divorced I really didn't have any money, and I had to learn all about the stock market. I had to save a lot of money. I was fifty-four years old when I started saving and in nine years I retired."

What retirement got her was the ability to relax and discover what she really wanted to do. Initially it meant joining a lot of different groups, which led her to think that she may have been trying to recreate the pace of her life in Chicago. She cut back and ended up with the feeling that she was more in control of her life than she'd ever been. Thinking about creativity has suggested she ought to look at painting.

She has had occasion to use the health care system locally for a TIA, (transient ischemic attack), something like a stroke event, but more transitory. She found the care very satisfactory and inexpensive. She has not elected to purchase Medicare Part B supplementary insurance and does not think that, short of a disastrous problem, she would go back to the States for treatment. She does not have Mexican health insurance. Her CAT scan for the

TIA cost $200 here. I have heard other figures as well that bear out the lower cost of medial treatment in Mexico. Forty dollars for x-ray, exam and cast for a broken arm. Seven hundred dollars for an emergency appendectomy with a three-day hospital stay.

Is San Miguel the answer for Marcia Loy?

"Mexico is certainly the answer. I'm going to Chiapas next month. I read somewhere that it may be the next San Miguel."

Digging for what might typify the San Miguel experience for her, Marcia comes up with the following anecdotes:

"Turning onto Umaran one day, which is not very wide, my wheel went up on a low wall. Before I could put it in reverse and gun it to back down, it went all the way over, so my wheel was spinning free. There were two guys walking by and there were three cars behind me, and two cars trying to come through once I get out of the way. Two of them are cab drivers, so seven guys got out, picked the car up and put it back on the street. I didn't have any money with me. I don't think they would have taken it, but I couldn't even offer any.

"A friend of mine was walking down the street and there was this little Mexican boy about ten years old and he was crying. So she asked him what was wrong, and he pointed up to the roof where his cat had jumped up. He couldn't get the cat to come down.

"My friend called a cab over and explained what had happened. The cab driver pulled up on the sidewalk and he got out, stood up on top of his cab, but he couldn't reach because he was short. So the cab driver and the little boy and my friend waited a few minutes and a real tall American came along. They explained to him what was wrong. He climbed on the top of the cab, but couldn't reach either. But then he picked up the little boy and held him up. "I mean, that's the kind of thing that happens here a lot." Her arms are spread wide as she finishes, as if to show that this place has enough heart for everyone.

What can she add, I ask, that might reveal something more about what she has learned from being here?

"The three most important things to Mexicans are [first] personal dignity—for even people like maids or garbage collectors, who in the States don't get a lot of respect, get it here. It's extremely important if you live here not to lose your cool with Mexicans, because you can't ever get it back. I've seen people do it and it's really ugly. Then, after personal dignity, are family and leisure time. In the family part I can see the goodness of it, but I also think it holds you back a lot. If you've got a brother-in-law who's an alcoholic and doesn't work, you've got to take care of his family. On the other hand, if you're old you don't get sent to the nursing home."

Or even to a trailer park in Keokuk, Iowa.

CHAPTER 18

THE LONG VIEW

Four generations of the Stark family have lived in San Miguel. The grandmother of Polly and C. C. came here in the 1960s to retire. Their parents joined her in the early 1970s, when the two girls were eleven and thirteen. Now they are both married and have five children between them. They know something about this place.

Tom McCanna is their cousin, a ceramic artist most recently from Cape Cod. His partner, Mark Baker, is the executive director of Hospice San Miguel, the only bilingual hospice organization in the Americas. Tom and Mark have been here nearly four years, Polly and C .C., thirty-five years. It's the anticipated contrast in their viewpoints that led me to risk trying to talk to all four of them at once.

"We were brought here as children," says C. C., "by our parents, but with the understanding that if we didn't fit in or weren't happy or comfortable, they would go somewhere else."

Their grandmother had consulted with other friends in the commercial illustration field before choosing San Miguel.

"When we visited for the first time," says Polly, "we being the Stark family, our parents were hooked."

"Our parents sold their house in suburban New York," adds C. C., "and initially were just living off the great exchange rate until they figured out how to educate us. It was a priority. They had to create their own school for us. My father, who was an artist, a painter, and when we left New York, a top textile designer with Fieldcrest Cannon, dropped all that and figured he could freelance from here.

"Being a kid here was stupendous," Polly says. "We had left the suburban New York lifestyle. TV was out of our lives. "

"They set up a home school situation and scoured the community for people who could act as teachers." The parents wanted to insure that the girls could reenter U.S. society and rejoin the school system at any point. As it played out, they didn't return until college. Polly didn't quite finish her art degree and returned after three years, but C. C., in California, finished and remained for five years before returning to San Miguel.

"I came down to visit the family in 1975," says Tom. "I was seventeen. I fell in love with it immediately. It's stayed with me all my life. We could go horseback riding, we could hang out in the *jardin*, we could go swimming up in the canyon, walk the pipeline. We'd go to the circuses. You'd meet people from all around the world. It was more of an international community. Right now it definitely feels like gringos versus Mexicans."

"The community of expats," adds Polly, "had chosen specifically to come here to write or to paint. There was an enormous group of poets."

"There would be lectures every week. There was much more community sharing in the arts than exists today," says Tom.

Polly makes a sweeping gesture around the garden where we sit. "And people lived in the little Mexican homes as they found them. There wasn't a sense of building new, or this needs to be fixed."

This is no "little" Mexican home, although it feels old. We are sitting in Mark and Tom's garden within their house on Calzada de la Luz. Behind us a mature tree sprouts stag-horn ferns from mossy nests, and toward the front, tall cypresses flank a large circular fountain. Pots hang everywhere, and other well-established trees crowd the neighbor's wall. Intense colors and decorative painting are everywhere. The garden is not quite out of control—you sense the force of Tom's mind behind it. Perhaps exuberant is the better word.

"The Instituto had wonderful classes in weaving, jewelry making, ceramics, sculpture," recalls Tom. "It was an incredible mix."

"The Stark family was a very artistic family," says Mark. "Tom, on his side of it, the McCanna family, is artistic as well. This was a natural draw for all of them."

"Our parents," says C. C., "knew how to motivate us to take on this new lifestyle and make the best of it. We didn't sit at home harping about what we left behind. We quickly forgot about many of our neighborhood friends. They became meaningless after the first year and a half."

Far from being a kid, Mark had left a career in health care management on Cape Cod. "Tom and I got together about twenty years ago, and I think our first trip here was 18 years ago. We came down to visit the family; Polly and C. C. and Uncle Bill and Aunt Alice." Before that Tom had been coming back every year or two since the first trip.

"Tommy and I would come down after that about every three years. We always thought about, well, some time in the future. I was working, and Tommy had his career."

"I was a ceramic artist, showing in New York and California."

"Every time we came down here we always got bit by the bug, just because of the color and the texture and the people. It just seemed more vibrant than—especially in the middle of winter—Cape Cod. Everything is black and white as opposed to color. It wasn't really until the second Bush election that we came for a friend's sixtieth birthday party and again got bit by the bug, and went back in January--it was as cold as all get out in Cape Cod—and I got on the computer for houses for sale by owner, and this one was there, and Tommy had actually had dinner in this house years before, and he knew the people who were here. And that's how we came to buy the house."

Was there a plan? Both were far from retirement age. They laugh at this. "I don't think we knew," says Mark. "Tommy's an artist. He can be an artist wherever he goes. I have no idea what I thought I was going to do. I thought maybe I'd write. Learning the language took the first seven months we were here."

Meanwhile Polly had come back to San Miguel and married her high school boyfriend. She had three children as she launched her painting career. C. C. returned after a 10-year absence and also married her Mexican boyfriend. She now has two kids.

"After three years in college," says Polly, "I was tremendously homesick for San Miguel, and Cleveland just wasn't cutting it. I have got to thank the dean of my department, who one day said to me, 'Polly, what are you doing here? Go back to Mexico. You don't need to be here, just go.' I've been a painter and muralist my entire career, and I've managed to see that all three of the kids have gone very successfully through college here in Mexico. Now they're working as artists."

Does being married to Mexicans give these two women an edge in connecting to the Mexican community? There is something like a muffled snort in response. "We got along famously," says C. C. "We learned the language quickly because we were so young. Running with the pack, we loved everything about Mexico."

"Most of the expats, when we moved here, were transients, people on sabbatical and so on," adds Polly. "We would make friends with their children, and nine months later these families would pick up and leave. We'd stay in touch for a couple of years by letter, and then we'd loose touch with them. After the first two or three years we did start to make very intense friendships with Mexicanos, especially men."

"Not boyfriends, just buddies," adds C. C.

"They were generally the lower working class. As much as we had our parents' friends saying, 'The girls should really be socializing with the so-and-sos,' we never did and we weren't attracted to it. Our buddies were the shoeshine kid, the boys playing basketball in the Parque Juarez. Their dads were gardeners."

"It's worth it," adds Tim, turning toward Polly, "to walk through town with these two, because you'll see who responds to them, who comes up and says hello. It's extraordinary. Because of the fact that you painted all the grand houses in San Miguel, it's like *Upstairs, Downstairs.* You know *all* the strata."

C. C. takes up this thread. "Our parents never tried to gear us to rub shoulders with any particular part of San Miguel society, like so many other gringos were encouraged to associate with the more affluent Mexican kids who were going to the country club."

I ask whether their husbands are well educated too.

"My husband did one year of college," says Polly.

"My husband did primary school, sixth grade," says C. C. "That's it."

Even today advancing beyond grade six is too great a hurdle for many kids, since government subsidies for uniforms and transportation end at that point and families are often just too poor to pick up the cost. I recall two or three years ago the mayor announcing proudly that the majority of San Miguel police were middle school graduates.

Fast forward to early 2005. Tom and Mark arrive to stay.

"We were incredibly fortunate," says Mark, "to have Polly, C. C., and their whole extended families to help us."

"We call them the *Sopranos* of San Miguel," adds Tom, "because things got done."

"For me it was traumatic. I had lived one semester abroad in Greece in my second year of college. That was it. The thought of Tommy and I actually packing up a three bedroom house from Cape Cod and moving 3,500 miles to central Mexico was frightening as all get out. We drove down and got here before the van." Because the house is in *centro*, they could not bring the big moving van in. Regulations forced them to unload everything into a bread truck on the outskirts and load into the house between ten P.M. and four A.M.

"We were extremely fortunate," continues Mark, "to have all of their contacts and long experience here, because they knew the plumber to call, they knew the electrician who would show up. They knew who did good work and who did bad, and what a fair price was."

"Which promises to believe, and which ones not to believe," adds C. C.

"Exactly. That made our position much more enjoyable. It was more of an adventure and less of a frightening experience. As soon as we unpacked, which took about four weeks, I went to school. I knew Tommy was probably not going to be the first one to learn Spanish, and I knew we had to. After that, I hit the streets, and that's when I got involved with Hospice. It coalesced at the same time."

Hospice San Miguel was in an organizational phase at that time. It was April of 2006. One of the directors, who knew Mark's background in health care administration, approached him and said that Hospice needed someone to put together policies and procedures. Mark had not worked here before that. "It was totally volunteer for about six months, and it was not my intention to go back to work. Eventually when they asked if I really want to work there, I said, 'Only if I'm legal.' They got me all my working papers."

Tom was working on the garden while this was going on. They had left his three ceramic kilns back in Provincetown. Tom had to figure out what he would do if he couldn't be working clay. "Now I'm doing wax and bronzes, other materials."

How have they changed, aside from hanging up their winter clothes?

"I'm just thrilled to enjoy the weather and grow things," answers Tom. "I was used to a zone seven planting schedule, and now this is zone nine. There are exotic things I can grow. But change wise? I can't compare it."

"For me," says Mark, "it's an unwinding of a wound-up clock. I'm still manic because that's part of my personality, but I'm less so. I'm much more available to the idea that if it doesn't get done today it'll get done tomorrow or the next day or the next day. That's very different from my lifestyle back on the Cape and in New York."

"One of the challenges to living in Mexico," says Polly, "that I think Tom has found tough, is the time it takes to get things done. You have an idea, you put it on paper—I'm talking about design ideas."

"There's an inertia that occurs down here," says Tom. "But we have designer friends from New York who fly down here. One of them is doing marble and alabaster lamp bases. We've been acting as a liaison for that kind of thing between businesses and designers. But that's our background too as a family."

Polly's painting is another example. "I am a decorative painter, a muralist. I've worked in San Miguel, in San Luis Potosi, over in Los Cabos for the $7 million homes over there. I do faux finishing as well."

"And C. C.'s the one in charge of the fireworks,"

says Tom, "and the tequila donkeys."

"My husband and I own a very small restaurant. It's down in the San Antonio neighborhood. He's the chef; he likes to cook. I'm in the events business. I'm a music and entertainment coordinator for weddings and parties. I work under the auspices of a lady here who has a business called Celebration San Miguel. Everything from guitar trios, mariachis, marimba bands to full salsa bands, Cuban bands. I'm a disc jockey for parties. I work with all kinds of fireworks for all events, working with the artisans who make exploding dolls."

It sounds like too much fun to ever think of going back.

"Never," she continues. "I think if I had to leave for economic reasons I would go elsewhere before I'd go back to the U.S. with my kids and my husband."

C. C. was just there with her husband on a visit. He had never been there before and she was relieved that he didn't fall in love with it.

"I haven't been back there for twenty years," says Polly. "But I just went to Canada for the first time, and I really liked it."

How about Mark and Tom? "I think," says Tom, "there's a different reality base when you live here full time instead of being here a few months out of the year. You get a sense of the seasons and the community."

"We do subscribe to [cable TV]," adds Mark. "We keep tabs on what's going on back there, especially with the last election, but I don't miss it at all. Barring an ill family member, nothing would make me go back. Even then I think I'd probably try to convince them to come down here instead. There's great health care here.

231

"You hear the story of the rat race that is America, and once you live here for a while, I have come to think that it really is a rat race back there. Everyone is so caught up in the latest trend or car or scandal. Here people are more interested in people and relationships and family. You don't need all the stuff the commercials tell you that you need."

"You can always tell," adds Tom, "*when* somebody moved here because that's their clothing, that's their fashion. You can time people because they don't get new clothes. You can freeze time with that. It was a men's clothing shop salesperson who observed that."

It's obvious to me that Polly and C. C. are different from most Americans I see here. There's a settled attitude in their manner and a style of speech that is three or four degrees off from standard colloquial American. Maybe it's speaking so much Spanish and not hearing much American media. Are they aware of it? And are they aware of being different from Mark and Tom?

"I think the most interesting point is that Polly and I are both to married to Mexican locals, and we're still married and raising kids, and happily married to our Mexican husbands. We didn't just fall in love with a hot, cute Latin guy and get pregnant and then everything fell apart. We've worked at our marriages, there have been challenges, but it's been fulfilling."

"I think it's funny," adds Polly, "what an American will consider being 'involved' in the Mexican community. 'We give them our money, we write them checks.' I think they have barely scratched the surface and often prefer it that way. A large number of the expats living here are very glad to have their American friends, and their circle. If they deal with the locals they deal mostly with the service providers, but there's no real depth."

I ask if she thinks the locals would welcome a deeper involvement. This is something I've heard differing views on. "More understanding, maybe," she says. "I think a lot of them would."

"I think C. C. and Polly are much more bicultural than Tommy and I," says Mark. "They've been here thirty-five years now. They know the saints' days, they know the fiestas, they know the families. We're newbies here. There was an old expression on Cape Cod that you're a wash-ashore even if you've been there for thirty years. Because you're really not a Portugee fisherman, and you'll never be one.

"I get exposed to it more because I'm working with a bilingual, bicultural staff. Seventy percent of our patients are Mexican. I still feel myself as an outsider."

"Here in San Miguel," adds Polly, "I can assume I am part of the community, but if I step out, we're as gringo as they come. We went to Leon with the kids to go iceskating, and when we stepped onto the ice all jaws dropped. A little waitress came up and asked where we're from."

C.C.'s children were recently in the States and loved Disneyland. Polly's have a different experience. "I have three kids, twenty-seven, twenty-six, and twenty-one. They are all Mexican by nationality. They were denied U.S. citizenship because we moved here when C. C. and I were young, and there's a law that requires individuals, if they have moved out of the U.S. before turning fourteen, to return to reside in the U.S. for three years before having their first child. They have to be able to prove it.

233

I have not or if I did [during college], I can't prove it. So when our son was born we took him in to Mexico City to register him at the embassy. He was denied U.S. citizenship." Upon finishing college first in his class as a young architect, the oldest, Alex, applied for a job in New York and was denied a visa. He now works in Canada.

"I'm a taxpayer, I'm a citizen," continues Polly, "and so this is an interesting twist. I also consider myself an American living with a Mexican family." C. C. does not have this problem because she lived in California for ten years before her children were born.

The changes they have seen since they came are too numerous to consider here, but among the more positive is that they are able to make a living in creative endeavors now that the town is more sophisticated. Mark and Tom, thinking back to their first visit eighteen years ago, lament the sprawl. It reminds them of the uncontrolled growth in the U.S. At the same time, most of this growth is fueled by the arrival of more Americans.

"Mexico is a surrealist country," says Tom, thinking of the constant appearance of the startling and the unexpected. "If you're an artist you can see that clearly and enjoy it. That's why so many creative people respond to it."

"Even as a nonartist," adds Mark, "what I enjoy about it is that it's taught me patience in life. You can take a deep breath and say, so if I'm stuck behind a garbage truck for five minutes and I can't get to work on time, it's OK. I've learned to take a breath and sit and look around for five minutes and see what I haven't seen. That's a gift, because I can remember rush hour in Boston."

I raise the issue of Mexican politics, not knowing

whether Polly and C.C. might have dual citizenship yet. "We can't vote," says C.C., "as close as we are to citizenship. Our husbands are very disgruntled with their country's politics. They don't trust anybody. Often they're not even interested in voting. They go from very angry to fully apathetic. At the same time they've been encouraged by what happened with Obama."

We haven't pursued many lines of discussion that we might have. I ask them to select one for comment. Polly takes this up.

"I think we're trying not to pound on the influx of people here. Who are we to comment? We're still washashores by your [Mark's] terms. Who are we to say who could or should come here?"

I suggest that everyone who comes down here wants to be the last one in. "I thinks that's true," says Mark. "I think there are some people who are very happy to just shut their doors [to all the others who might follow] and live in the sanctity of their four walls and garden."

"But bring us the eccentrics, bring us the people that really want to mix," injects C.C.

"I would say," says Mark, "the scariness I felt before I moved down here, it's turned out to be the best adventure I've ever taken in my adult life."

CHAPTER 19

MOVING ON, LOOKING BACK

W hat happens when it doesn't completely work?

When it's right in almost every way, but not in one or two that are critical? I don't mean personal health issues or the needs of a failing parent. Someone told me San Miguel was a place where people often hit the wall after five or seven years. I have listened for that sound, the thud of flesh against old masonry, as I wander about looking for people to talk to, but I haven't heard it.

I *have* heard the reluctance to talk of several people who are leaving and feel odd about it, or who are not leaving and wish they were.

One who is leaving and was willing to have a wistful conversation about it is Jody Feagan. She first came with her three children to give them an opportunity to learn Spanish and experience a culture different from their own. A conscientious mother, she had no way of knowing that her children would end up living in an orphanage.

"We were living in Nashville, and it was hot for the summers and we wanted to take a break. I looked for schools that accepted small children and we found one here that took children at age two, and that was my youngest at the time, so that's how we ended up here." That youngest child, Wyatt, is now eleven. They had never been to San Miguel, but Jody and her husband didn't look anyplace else.

"After I found out about that school taking children that young," says Jody, "I started doing a little research, and we came down the November prior to the year we moved here just to see the city. My husband and I came down so I had a chance to get my bearings, because I would be here on my own with the kids, and then my husband would come back and forth from work."

It was 1999 and none of them spoke Spanish. Initially it was only for the following summer. But two years later when they decided to sell their house in Nashville and move, a lot of eyebrows went up.

"Our friends thought we were crazy. We had rented here for the first two years, not in this house. Then we came down for a school year and rented for that year. We had a great year. I felt like it was a wonderful place to be for my kids. I wasn't sure where we wanted to go next. My husband has a job that allows him to be flexible about where he can be."

Then they found the house that became their home. It was the sixteenth century ruin of the town orphanage, and it had given its name to the street: Hospicio. Of course it had no roof at all and some of the walls had collapsed. A realtor in the States would have called it a fixer-upper.

"We fell in love with it and decided to buy it and make it our permanent residence."

We are sitting in the central dining area for this

conversation, a long barrel-vaulted room with a kitchen at one end and a sitting area at the other. Outside, a central courtyard faces walls on all sides of both new and old stone. Many of the old interior walls were seamlessly incorporated into the design. You have the sense of a selective decay that left a marvelous set of rooms and spaces crisp and inviting. Not even the kids mind living in *this* orphanage.

"I loved it here. I felt it was great place to raise my children. It's a small community; I feel very safe. It's a very international community, the kids in their schools are from all over the world. I love the pace here. I just feel like it's a wonderful way to live. You take time each day to just enjoy life, instead of commuting."

To the kids, Jody portrayed the move as an adventure, and they were enthusiastic about it. They were too young to have the kind of attachments to their friends that would have caused a problem.

At this point the oldest boy, Connor, has gone on to high school at the Milton Academy in Boston. Jody didn't feel that the high school options in San Miguel were challenging enough. "They don't have a science lab in their school. After he got the Spanish, I felt like he needed a whole lot more in terms of academics. He's in a school of elite academic [qualifications]. Robert Kennedy went there, T. S. Eliot went there. Connor has done biochemistry and forensic science in the Johns Hopkins summer programs."

A noise interrupts us, coming from above. It's the retractable roof, says Jody. In the old days, all the orphans would have made a run for it.

I am getting the sense from this that their pending

departure is about the kids, but I'm still more focused on the early part of their stay. Was it about what Mexico was? Or were they getting away from something?

"I feel like it—and I still do even though we're going to go back for our children to go to school—but as soon as we get a chance, we'll come back here. I love the people, I love the way you are walking somewhere and stopping to say hello to your neighbors. Meeting someone for coffee to talk about business or an event, versus e-mails and faxes. I can't remember last time I put money on my cell phone. For me it's enriched my life and my children's lives."

Jody has been for a long time one of the major guiding forces behind organized writing activities in San Miguel. I am always interested in how people connect with the community here, whether the Mexican or the expatriate side.

"I have a journalism degree and I worked in radio and television. I stopped working when I had my children, so I haven't worked for pay for almost sixteen years. When I got here I didn't have any intention of making a career. But then I met Beverly D'Onofrio. She was a writer here and a good friend, and she wanted to teach a workshop, but all she wanted to do was show up and teach, she didn't want to do all the preparation for it and deal with payment and organizing and publicizing. So we partnered on that and it's worked great, and I still produce her workshops about once a year.

"From there I had other authors and teachers come to me and want to teach something while they were here. Then I continued the process of organizing other writing workshops, and I came up with the idea to do a writer's conference, where we had an annual event where we brought in a name author. I had met with Susan Page, and I was on the founding board of the Authors' Sala."

Now, with her departure imminent. Jody approached Susan Page about the having the Authors' Sala take over the writers' workshops. Early in 2008 she and Susan jointly founded the Literary Society as a fund raising arm of the Authors' Sala. With these additional funds it will be possible to hold more events like writers' conferences. This past summer novelist Tom Robbins was a big success at such a conference.

I suggest that walking away from this kind of effort must be almost the hardest part of leaving. "It's sad that I have to leave, but with the Writers' Conference I still intend to be very much a part of it, like this year [2009] I'll come back in February and get everything in place. I taught myself how to design the websites because at the time we couldn't afford to pay anybody to do it. I'll still be able to do the websites and all the e-mail marketing. We have a good group of people that volunteer. I still think I'll be able to be involved."

At this point, after a winter school semester in Aspen, Jody and the kids will probably be living for a while in the condo in Los Angeles that Jordan Feagan bought after they sold their Nashville house. "His main business for the last fifteen years has been as a sports agent. He represents NFL players and major league baseball players." Because of his job demands he was able to work for extended periods from San Miguel, but was never able to live here full time.

They are keeping the San Miguel house on Hospicio, using it for a combination of house trades and rental.

After the youngest, Wyatt—now about to enter grade six—finishes high school, Jody plans to return to San Miguel full time. "Definitely. It feels like home to me. This will always be a place, too, that my kids will feel is their home and come back to."

It isn't that she hasn't been pleased with the education the kids have had here, but besides the absence of a science lab, it has some of the limitations of the small town schoolhouse.

"I think there are about forty students, but that's from fifth to twelfth grade. It's tiny. For some kids that's wonderful. I just feel that as mine have gotten older at some point they need more of a high school experience, and they're excited about it. Kirby is [entering grade nine] and she's very much looking forward to going to football games or school dances. There's not the population here to do that."

Thinking about returning to the U.S. is naturally a time to think about how things have changed in Jody's own outlook. "I think I have a broader view of the U.S. now because being outside looking in you get other people's points of view. You see how the world sees the United States. I feel now more educated about things. I don't know if it's apathy, but you feel like when you're in the middle of it you almost don't see what's going on. I have a better sense now of what our role is in the world."

But does she feel this shift in perspective will make it difficult to be back for a period of years as the kids finish school?

"I'm the type of person that can look at the situation and figure out the best parts of it and enjoy them. For example, we spent eight weeks in Los Angeles this past summer. It's very different from San Miguel, and I just focused on all the things that San Miguel didn't have that I could enjoy. There was a great art theater that we could walk to, and fantastic restaurants. The library was fabulous. I had to drive a lot, which was not good. We went to the beach every week. You can't allow yourself to go, 'Oh, I have to be in this traffic and smog, and all these people. I have to drive everywhere and it's so expensive.' I think it's just how you focus on things."

The Feagans have known for some time that this move was coming, so it's no surprise, yet it requires some emotional preparation for Jody, feeling as she does about San Miguel. "Thinking about living somewhere else, I see it as an adventure. You embrace that and look forward to what you'll learn or discover. But I feel like this is such a special place that when I'm here I feel like this is home."

I sense there's a price to this. Not every place, whether beautiful or interesting arouses these feelings.

"I feel like I'm going to lose some of my identity leaving here. It's a lot of things. I feel like the literary conference and workshops, that was something I conceived of and started on my own, and it's been successful. It's been an interesting adventure that I started. When I get introduced a lot of times people will say I'm part of the Authors' Sala or the Writers' Conference. It's how I'm recognized in the city. I've created that identity for myself.

"When I'm somewhere other than here people are fascinated by the fact that I took my children and moved to Mexico. It's a unique and interesting thing, and people always want to know about it and how it's worked. That won't be me anymore either. I will have done that, but I won't be doing it. I'll lose a lot of that."

242

The list goes on for some length. For Jody it is not only about identity, it is also about how to reconstruct the components of her entire day in the absence of the dance classes, the Tai Kwon Do, aerobics, the two years she taught Shakespearean theater, and the interactions with the dozens of friends she encounters in this small town on any walk down the street. "I've made my mark in a lot of ways in this community. I feel like I've helped enrich San Miguel, and in return it's been very enriching for me."

As she herself changed over this so time so has the town.

"I guess it's been good and bad, like the big Mega supermarket. To me, I find that's convenient. They didn't allow it in *centro*, which is very much still the original co- lonial city. I used to have to go to Querétaro once a week and do a big shop. The less I have to drive in my car--I've maybe put $20 worth of gas in the car in the last month--I rarely drive and I love it.

"It's convenient to have a good movie theater here as well, for my kids. In terms of *centro*, there's more traffic. That's noticeable. The Vonnage phone, the wire- less Internet, allow my husband to work here eight or ten days at a time and then travel. When we first moved here we had to go to Internet cafes."

Jody is less certain how much she has changed herself. "I'm probably less stressed. I have a lot of help. With my husband traveling a lot, to have a full time cook and a maid allows me to have time for myself. When the kids get home from school I can focus on their needs. Most of their activities they can walk to. I'm not the constant soccer mom, driving around, which is a reality of your life in the States."

It's almost pointless to ask whether she would do this again.

"In a heartbeat. It's one of the best things we've ever done in our lives. One of my best friends in Nashville couldn't imagine why I wanted to do this, and finally she came down to visit, and she walked into our house and said, 'OK, now I get it.' I think one of the reasons this town feels so welcoming to the people who live here and friendly and accepting is that people chose to be here, chose to make their life here, and are happy about that choice. If you're somewhere and feel stuck, of course that affects your attitude, but if you're here because this is where you want to be, you walk down the street with a smile. It radiates to everyone else too."

Once here, getting inside the culture was easier for Jody than for some others. The key was her children. "When your children are little, you meet all the moms and do lots of play groups, and most of those parents that I met through the first years of school were Mexican. I had a very strong desire to learn the language and not just have American friends. That's easy to do here."

Did this lead to having close Mexican friends?

"Yes, and I still do. They're still good friends of mine even though our kids have separated and gone to different schools."

But like others, Jody could not say that they are in the first tier of her friends. Yet she feels that four years ago she would have given a different answer.

I left this conversation with the feeling that Jody has arrived at a balanced and relaxed view of her coming departure. Possibly her clear intention to return after the school process is finished for her children makes this easier.

Keeping the house on Hospicio anchors it. San Miguel has given her family a great deal, and it is Jody's style to have given much back.

CHAPTER 20

GOING HOME, BUT IS IT?

Tiburon, California, is a great place to live. Full of quaint old homes and many upscale new ones, its location at the northern end of San Francisco Bay places it in the path of fresh breezes and delightful views. It feels at once close in and restfully remote. Depending on traffic, the Golden Gate Bridge is sometimes five minutes away. Ferries will take you anywhere around the Bay. The squawk of gulls suggests Nantucket. Looking in from the outside, it resembles nothing so much as the American Dream.

Yet for their $320,000 annual income, Dave Richards and his wife, Diane, found themselves on a treadmill, running in place, unable to save for their two children's education or for their own retirement. Never daring to slow down, they worked so many hours they felt like they had hired other people to raise their children. The sky above was filled with clean, fresh air, but they couldn't breathe. Yet Tiburon, California, is a great place to live.

Property taxes on their home were $1,200 a month. Mortgage payments were another $5,000. It cost $2,000 a month to keep their two children in preschool. Income taxes took more than 40% of their wages. After food, clothing, insurance, and two cars, the cash remaining was unimpressive. Was this the American Dream? And why did it seem at times like a nightmare from which they couldn't awaken?

"The idea came to my wife and me," says Dave Richards, "that living in the Bay Area was not going to work for the long term. We didn't want to raise our children there. There were two main issues. One was the cost of living. My wife was making what I considered phenomenal money, $200,000 plus. I was making over $100,000. For the past few years we had been disgusted by the fact that we made that much money and yet our lifestyle had grown to absorb that much money. We couldn't afford to not make that much money, and we couldn't live without it. We were saving very little. We would put $100 a month in a 401K or $50 in the kids' college fund.

"More important than anything was that we found ourselves in a situation where we were both working long hours and paying other people to raise our children. That's really where the crux of the matter was. I was leaving the house at six o'clock in the morning and getting home at seven or seven-thirty."

For this conversation Dave and I are sitting in my *sala*, my San Miguel living room. It's the first time anyone has come here for these talks. I prefer to sit in their homes to see how they live, but today Dave is running from one business appointment to another, and I caught him as he ran past. He's a tall man with an athletic build and ruddy complexion. Eager to tell his story, he talks rapidly with broad gestures and much feeling. It's already starting to sound like a cautionary tale.

Over his shoulders, through my arched windows,

I watch the 16-foot bamboo climbing the back wall of my patio as he pauses for breath. I found Dave through his posting on the Internet, trying to find a good placement for his nanny. His wife and kids have already gone back over the border, so I know where this is going. I ask if it was the hope of a more economical lifestyle that drew them to San Miguel.

"My wife used to say it was a chance for us to step off the treadmill of the rat race. We looked over the kitchen at each other one night and said, this is how it's going to be for the next eighteen years. Our children were two and four. It wasn't like we were just going to have to work hard for two more years and then it's over. There were eighteen more years of *this*, of stress, of long hours, of making $320,000 a year and not saving anything, and God, I hope our house is worth five million when we decide to retire because that's the only thing we have of value."

Dave was the director of operations for a company that provided high speed Internet. Diane Richards was a senior art director in advertising.

The first tentative thought of escape was to look for a place in the U.S. where they could live on the earnings of just one of them. They wanted to recover the way each of them had grown up. Their mothers hadn't worked. At the end of the school day, someone was there to come home to. Perhaps one of their jobs could translate into a calmer lifestyle in a more moderately priced location. Maybe it could still be the American Dream.

"Both those jobs are high stress. I can't tell you how many times on a Friday afternoon at four o'clock her boss would walk into her office and say, 'Hey, we've got a

big presentation on Monday. I hope you don't have anything planned for this weekend.' When you're twenty-sev-
en and single and you're making 200 grand a year that's
not a problem. But when you've got a two year old and a
four year old, you want to be home with your children.

"We started looking at places like Bend and Port-
land, Oregon. We looked at places outside of Albuquer-
que and Las Cruces. Little places that had some high tech,
had a college. We looked at the research triangle in North
Carolina, but found it had already been discovered. I had
never heard the name San Miguel de Allende. My wife
had friends who had bought a house down here. They
had done very well in the Silicon Valley boom of the late
90s."

Dave had gone to high school in Santa Barbara.
He knew from experience that Mexico had beaches where
you could get cheap beer. He spoke virtually no Spanish,
but had fond memories of the place and thought the beer
was good. Diane had always loved Mexico, and they'd
had a mariachi band at their wedding. But neither had
ever been to the interior; it was always the typical beach
vacations.

The Silicon Valley friends of Diane had come to
San Miguel for a wedding and bought a house that weekend. "They bought a place by the park. They had told
us about it: 'You should come down and visit us.' I didn't
know where San Miguel was. It's not by the ocean. It
doesn't sound like that much fun to me. I don't just jet off
to these Mexican weekends like people with money do."

This is a telling statement. They're just scraping
by on 320K a year. But one of the friends knew a woman
who owned a voice over Internet business [like Skype or

Vonnage] and was having some technical difficulties. She connected the two by phone, and Dave was persuaded to come down and help out for a couple of days. Diane urged him to go. He was unenthusiastic at the idea. "I had never seen a picture of it, I'd never gone on the Internet to look at it. I didn't know what it was. I was stunned. Last time I was in Mexico I was in Cabo San Lucas, which is like a poor man's Vegas. I hated it. The abject poverty next to five star hotels with a dead donkey in the street. The $7 beers by the pool.

"We worked all day in her office, which is right by the *jardin* [the main Plaza]. She took me out to lunch. We walked around and I was thinking, this is one of the most beautiful little towns. All of a sudden it started clicking. Maybe I could be a voice over IP consultant? All her clients are Americans. I was stunned when I found out there were all those Americans who lived here. They'd found a little treasure.

"Two days later I flew back home. I'd spent a day walking around. It's such a cliché, but I fell in love with it. I went back and I told my wife. She basically said, 'Please have fun in Mexico. My divorce lawyer will contact you. Send the alimony checks my way and visit the children whenever you want. Because not in a million years will I take my children to Mexico to live. I'm certainly not taking them to central Mexico, where people get kidnapped and there's a lot of crime and it's horrible and they're going to die of cholera. Trust me on this one, Dave, it's not going to happen.'

"I said, 'All I want you to do is spend one weekend down there, and I will never mention it again. Period.'

"The next cliché, of course, is that the second

day we're here she's frantically calling elementary schools trying to arrange tours. She's like, 'What do mean you're not open on Sundays? I need to come and look at your school and interview your teachers!' It was literally the second day. She fell hard."

The woman who had needed help on her Internet business introduced them to another woman who had two children. They were invited to a birthday party at her house. "They lived in Candelaria, a gated community outside of San Miguel, and they'd invited all the kids from the school.

"Before came down here, Diane had done some research on the Internet. It came up as a lot of old people, a lot of blue hairs, it's basically a retirement community for wealthy Americans and a few hippies. She also hit some blogs from bitter people who'd left here. After that she was prepared not to like it. But San Miguel is such a special place that it will turn the hearts of people who come here thinking, 'This is not for me.' So we went to this birthday party for a three-year-old, and it was full of young parents, just like us. The were people who had run away from the rat race. You had a few Mexicans who worked really hard so that they could send their kids to private school. It was a nice, fun mix. There was a lot of alcohol and it was a beautiful house. Candelaria is this gorgeous little gated community with a swimming pool and staff serving you ice-cold beers and margaritas, and Diane's sitting there like, 'Are you kidding? This is ridiculous.'

"She was sold. She said, 'Why are we looking at Bend, Oregon? Las Cruces, New Mexico? Charleston, South Carolina?'"

Of course I understand the charm myself, but

I can't stop looking at the money part of this. "What happened," I ask, "when Diane walked away from her $200,000 job?"

"Well, there were a lot of late night talks. The next question was how can we make money down there, and that's when I felt the hand of fate sort of push me. At that moment the woman who owned the ISP said to me, Dave, 'I want to sell the company.' So I'm thinking, here's a small company for sale."

The growth potential was clear. The owner was overextended with the demands of another business and had family problems as well. There was no one in San Miguel who knew this business the way Dave did. It was one of those turning point moments.

"There were many heart-to-heart conversations with my wife, but we felt like this was a place that solved some problems. The cost of living was drastically lower. We had the ability to make money. With a tiny bit of money I could buy a company that had great growth potential. Don't forget, this is four years ago. There's no economic downturn. There's no trouble on the horizon. People are building like mad. This town was booming."

Dave's cell rings. It's one of his employees, and Dave's Spanish sounds like he grew up here. He could be a smooth gringo villain in a bad Mexican crime movie, the kind you'd never see north of the border.

"The thing I'm most proud of is my Spanish and my children's Spanish. If I'm taking nothing out of Mexico, I speak another language, not perfectly, but I have good skills and my children are pure Mexican native speakers. My daughter is a Mexican."

Before they left California they agreed they would

not sell their house in Tiburon. "If we have to flee Mexico because we hate it," Diane said, "I want a place to go."

They rented a place with three bedrooms in the Guadiana neighborhood for $800 a month. There was a big yard for the kids, who were enrolled in a private Montessori school. Dave and Diane's income had dropped by 90%, but it was OK.

"We thought, this is it, we'll be here for seven or eight years. And nothing bad has happened. I'm leaving San Miguel sadly. I would like to stay here for a lot longer. I love it here. But it really comes down to money.

"My business when I bought it was barely turning a profit, but there was good growth potential. We tripled the business, cut the costs, we've streamlined it. It makes about forty grand a year now. That's not bad, but here's what I find. It's hard to make money in Mexico. It is not a country that is friendly to small business. Less than one percent of the population has controlled the money and the real estate and everything else for a long time."

What are the specifics of this? It's hard to imagine that in the voice over ISP area Dave was going to have much local competition.

"The larger I grow the more barriers I come up against, and the only way I can overcome them is through corruption and bribery and *mordidas* [payoffs], and hiding from the government and doing business in a black market fashion. By sidestepping laws and customs. I have to smuggle equipment into Mexico because I can't bring it in legally. If I bring in a $100 piece of equipment I have to pay $240 in customs, so now that piece of equipment is $340. I have to sell it for $500 to make a profit, but it's still a $100 piece of equipment back in the States. So people are saying, 'Why am I paying $500 for a piece of equipment I just saw at [a Stateside electronics discounter] for 90 bucks?' So they just won't buy it.

"Because I'm in telecommunications, I have to do business with Telmex. By law you cannot send data out of Mexico unless it goes through Telmex's hands. So all my customers, their e-mails, their websites, everything else, goes through Telmex. Telmex charges me exorbitant rates for my bandwidth. The more bandwidth I need the more I have to pay. It's at the point where I can barely afford to resell it. In the United States the bigger your company gets the more clients you have, but in Mexico the more clients you have your costs rise at an even rate, so if you have a thousand clients you make forty grand or if you have a hundred clients you make forty grand. The more gross you make the higher you get in the tax brackets and you pay ridiculous taxes. You have to start hiding your money from the government.

"I don't like to hide, and I don't like to live in fear. I'm not comfortable living with three children where if the phone rings I might be in trouble. But if I did it legally, I'd pay all my money in taxes. So what do I do? Do I go bankrupt and flee the country? Or do I play the game that most Americans play down here where they hide money. I have two accounts: I have a *factura* account and a non-*factura* account. A *factura* is a legal receipt. It's required by law. If you do any financial transaction for profit you have to have a *factura*.

"Most of my clients are Americans. If you bought my service, would you need a legal receipt? No, you don't need one, so I'm not going to give you one. That money is now under the table. It's illegal money. If 90% of your transactions are in cash, as mine are, it gets you into a very gray area. That's one thing.

"Here's the other thing. The cost of living here is not that cheap. It's much cheaper than New York City or San Francisco, but it's not like living in Oaxaca or Chiapas, or Guatemala. You're not going to buy a house here that's nice for $100,000. The gringos have arrived. Go to Mega and feed three kids. You're not coming out of there with cheap groceries.

"My company makes enough money to live on, but we put nothing away. We had a child here. I'm 47 years old with three kids, the oldest of which is seven, and the youngest is nine months. I don't put away anything for their college, and I'm not putting away anything for my retirement. It's all in the house in Tiburon, which has now lost value, by the way. That house is never going to plummet, and I'll have some money left over. If I wait five, six or seven years I'm going to be OK. But at the same time, I'm not saving anything, and I'm not comfortable with that.

"We're starting to get a little worried. How long are we going to be able to do this? I'm going to be fifty-five in eight years. I'm not really hirable then. I'm in high tech and I've been out of the country for ten years at that point. Right in the middle of that uncertainty, which is not enough to drive us out of San Miguel, because we both love it, my wife gets a job offer that is her dream job. My children, all their best friends are Mexicans. My daughter—she's blond and blue eyed—if a Mexican heard her, he would think that she's a Mexican, too.

"So, here's my wife's dream job. She gets an offer from Apple computer. A good friend of hers works there, calls her up and says, Diane, there's a job that's coming open in two weeks. You are perfect for it. We're going to try to find a person exactly like you and hire her.'"

Diane brings this message to Dave. You can imagine the conflicted look on her face. He's not ready to go back to the rat race. They would have to live in Cupertino because, being at the opposite end of San Francisco Bay, a commute from their house in Tiburon is out of the question.

"I said yes, we're struggling a little bit, but the salary they're offering her is $425,000 a year. In this market, in this economic downturn. She goes up and she has eleven interviews, three a day. Ending with sitting in a conference room with eight executive vice presidents and Steve Jobs, who doesn't say a word through the whole interview. It's pretty daunting stuff. My wife is an ass-kicker. They send her a letter that says we want you, you need to start Monday. This is on a Thursday. What do you do?

"You don't want to go back to the rat race, but you're not making any money. They guarantee her a year. Her friend, who's been there ten years, says, 'Diane, everyone loved you. They were raving about you. They'll want you to stay. It's yours to lose.'" Dave pauses here and looks me in the eye. "You help me out, John. As a life coach, what do you do?"

So much for being a fly on the wall. There's no way out that I can see. Diane can go up and work without the rest of them, but it separates the family. The kids are too young for this, and because of the hours Dave works, they'd end up being raised by strangers again. Besides, Dave would still have his concern about the tax people here asking awkward questions, and the risk is weighing him down. And without the Apple job, they're all still running in place; it's just a place they like better than Tiburon, or probably, Cupertino. How ironic that their unpalatable alternative is to take a very high paying dream job and move to California.

"The whole thing gets down to the kids and your age," I tell him. "If you were older and if the kids were on their own and finished with college..."

"It would be a no-brainer."

"As it is, you can't pass it up."

"Many, many hours there were tears, there were talks. We didn't sleep. It always came back to, 'this is going to give us a chance [to make headway] for the first time. Not only that, we're going back to a situation where we're a lot wiser. We're not going to go back to San Jose and buy a $1.5 million house. We've rented a house for $2,000 a month. We're going back *frugal*. We know frugal now because we've been in Mexico for three years. We thought we knew what it was when we lived in Marin County, surrounded by Range Rovers and I drove a new Ford truck because I wanted to be frugal. You live there surrounded by multimillionaires and you think you know what frugal is. Frugal is, 'Not the Italian marble counter tops, we're just going to go with the domestic marble counter tops when we remodel our kitchen *again*.' That's what *was* frugal.

"Now it's like none of that matters. We're going to go with the linoleum. We're going with a *white* refrigerator. We're not going with the big, stainless steel aircraft carrier barbecue."

I suggest that this means they are coming back different people—nothing short of that.

"We're coming back completely different people, with completely realigned objectives."

But exactly how are they different? What's the detail?

"Here's what we take away from Mexico. What's important is how much time you spend with your kids. How happy are your kids? How well adjusted are they? How well behaved are they? And the better behaved they are is almost always a key to how much time their parents spend with them. Poorly behaved kids grow up with maids and nannies who don't really discipline them, don't really teach them the core values that your parents taught you." I am instantly reminded of one of Dave's opening lines, that he and Diane felt they were paying other people to raise their kids.

"Another thing is that what we thought was frugal was wildly extravagant and immaterial. Now we realize that you can live simply and still have a fantastic life. It doesn't matter what kind of counter tops you have, it matters who's gathered around the counter tops. If you had talked to me the day before we moved down here, I would have told you we lived a fairly frugal life, we lived within our means. Now I look back on my life and I shudder at the abundance and the extravagance of our lifestyle. At what I thought was under control and it wasn't. I was very materialistic and very consumerist. I leave Mexico shunning consumerism and materialism."

In their earlier life had they found meaning in this or was it simply the way everyone around them thought?

"To be honest I think it was some of both. I felt that when you had children it was important to surround them with quality things. It was important to have a house

that was immaculate and all their toys to be super sophisticated, because when they went to their friend's house
that's what they were playing with.

"In Mexico I find that children are growing up
happy and they have never seen anything like that. They
play with rocks. How about one soccer ball for ten kids?
They'll play all day and they'll come back exhausted,
physically fit, happy within their group, and learning
how to work among themselves. You play soccer for six
hours you're going to have some disagreements with your
peers."

What are they dreading about going back?

"I'm dreading crawling back into a long commute, and the traffic and the road rage. The whole idea
of stress and work, work, work. I've committed to myself
to not fall back into that. Because of Diane's salary I can
chose work that gives me flexible hours. I can take my
kids to school and pick them up. I'm committed to that.
It might be me doing that for the next ten years, and I'm
OK with that."

What is the main reason for going back?

"It's that ten years from now, when I'm in my late
fifties, I'm going to be able to do things and provide a secure financial network for my kids. If they choose to go to
college I'll be there. I think if we stay here, that's not going
to be possible."

I ask if he's concerned that the kids will readopt
that old value system. After all, by his own account they've
already become Mexicans in less than four years. Wouldn't
the process work both ways?

"I don't think so. I can't say I'm without concerns,
but I can also say that I'm so hypersensitive to it that I

think with my supervision and application of values on a daily basis, I can steer them a little bit. I think children are hardwired. You're not going to make a shy boy extroverted and you're not going to make an extroverted boy shy, but you can show your children what's important and what's not. When you're living a lifestyle of abundance and consumerism, they're going to see that. When you're not, the kids will see the difference."

Dave and Diane plan to return to Mexico once the youngest, now nine months old, has entered college. They own two one-acre lots in San Miguel. The property taxes total $85 a year. His company is for sale. He considered trying to keep the business long distance, but that presents problems. He feels his employees are the best he's ever had in terms of hard work and honesty, but while he doesn't like to generalize about Mexican workers, he feels that they lack the stand up ability to improvise if a critical situation should arise in his absence. "They are employees that, given a clear job description, will perform their duties magically and wonderfully, but won't proactively seek out opportunities or react to change well. That's my experience."

He's talking to three potential buyers, and I can see this might be hard for him. He rebuilt the business from a failing condition, and there is real pride in that, but it was also the thing that was to sustain the Richards family in their new life. It didn't, so how does he field this emotionally?

Dave subsides a bit and sinks into himself. It was easier talking about the kids. "It's bittersweet. It's more sad than anything else. I feel a little twinge of guilt, but that's too strong a word. I feel like I wish I had known more before I came to Mexico, I wish I had been able to make my decision based on the reality of owning a business in Mexico. You come down here and it's a little bit of a false economy.

"I think the majority of the people that come down here have some money. The average San Miguel person is not rich, but they sold their house for $700,000 and then they spent $300,000 here and put $400,000 in the bank. Let's be honest, if you live in Mexico and you put $400,000 in the bank, you're pretty wealthy. I don't consider that wealthy in the United States. You live in Manhattan and you have $400,000 in the bank you can live for two years. But down here, you can have $1,000 a month from social security, or maybe you're a teamster and you've got $1500 a month coming in. If you live simply you can probably do it on $20,000 a year, if you don't have three kids.

"I wish I had known that, Dave, you're not going to be able to make the money you think. It's going to cost you more than you think. Do you still want to do it, knowing that you're not going to make eighty, live for thirty and put fifty grand a year away for retirement? That's the reality, I thought. That wasn't the picture that it ended up being.

"However, the picture it ended up being was better, because I learned about the Mexican people, and without speaking Spanish you're never going to learn about living here. Do whatever you have to do, but learn it. It's a nuanced language, a subtle language. That's your ticket into society.

"I have a slight regret that I wasn't able to engineer a life where I could live simply and make enough money to save a little more. I almost feel like Mexico was an insurmountable challenge. I couldn't climb that mountain."

Did Diane have the same regrets?

"I think she looked forward more to leaving and with less sadness than I have. She developed two close friendships here with Mexican women; they're her best friends. Both have spent a lot of time in the United States. They're married to men who worked in the States. My wife does not speak Spanish; she cannot converse. My three best friends, that I spend a lot of time with, don't speak English. That changes things for me."

Something else occurs to me. Diane has gone toward something, Dave is leaving something. His willingness to speak so freely about his coming loss makes me ask if he has something to say directly to those who are staying here.

He looks at me for a moment, gathering his thoughts. I can tell that he sees it as going farther than a parting comment. It's more like a summing up. "Here's what I would tell them. Mexico has many great things going for it, and a lot of things that will drive an American berserk. There are plenty of negatives to distract you from the wonderful life you have here. But do not let them distract you.

"Never forget that you live in an esthetically pleasing place, filled with the most friendly and wonderful people, the best foods, the freshest fruit, the best weather, the most relaxed lifestyle, the highest quality of life. Do not let the few things that are difficult in Mexico, the *topes* (speed bumps), the petty government officials who make things hard, the wrong store hours posted--these are all things that will mean less and less the longer you live in Mexico. After you are gone, you are going to miss the great things more than you are happy to be away from the not-so-great things."

Amen. I can't help but think Dave is speaking to himself as well as to us.

I wish I didn't see a cloud hanging over this, but as a parent of young adults myself, I wonder whether the Mexican values the Richards' kids now have can be preserved back in the States, despite Dave's example and determination. What I found was that as my own kids got older the example of their peers overpowered mine. In any case, I wish the Richards well and I hate to see them leave.

CONCLUSIONS

I could go on and on. There are as many stories here as there are people. The next one would probably go something like this:

Several things were not quite right when Tom Sprague bought his 300-year-old San Miguel mansion in 1977. One was the collapsed ceiling in one of the bedrooms. Another was the skeleton and bloody dagger buried under the tile floor of one of his bathrooms. Fixer-uppers are often a challenge here. You can hire a house inspector, but they don't always catch every detail.

What a great opener, I thought when I heard this story, but the conversation never happened. It was one of thousands that never happened. The broad differences in viewpoint just among the conversations that *did* happen suggest how vast the range might be. The principal thing that people who came here have in common is that they came here. Not much more.

When I started this project it was suggested to me that my process was unscientific, my conclusions would lack validity, and my sample would have no statistical significance. I was undeterred. This book aims at a general audience and attempts to prove nothing.

My task was simpler: to provide my reader, a person I imagined was planning to move to Mexico, or at least fantasizing about it, with a means of getting inside the heads of people who had done it. I wanted to examine the process that led to the move, the difficulties of pulling it off, the contrast between expectations and reality, and the personal changes that came about because of it. Toward end of the book, I wanted to talk with people for whom it didn't work, or mostly worked but not in some key ways. The place has its drawbacks, and it's not for everyone.

I chose San Miguel as the focus of this book because I live here and I know it better than any other part of Mexico. It is not representative in every way. The real estate is expensive because the market is driven by Americans and Canadians who have settled here. It does not attract the beach people, but it does draw those looking for a more genuine experience of old Mexico. Some will argue that the presence of more than 5,000 gringos here distorts the mix, and I'm sure it does. But at the same time, the gringos provide a critical mass that gives support to newcomers, vast assistance to charitable groups, and an economic base that furnishes thousands of jobs. The pharmacist, veterinarian, or architect you use here was probably educated by scholarships provided by gringos.

There are jazz and chamber music festivals, theater, numerous art galleries, educational opportunities in all areas, as well as fine restaurants and hotels. The makings of true quality of life are readily at hand.

While I did search for variety in those I talked to, I made no attempt to be demographically correct. I saw my role as guiding the conversations. I wanted to be more than a fly on the wall, but not a discussion group leader. While the book was never about me, there were times when I did step forward and highlight some issues that I thought from my own experience were more important than others.

I began the interviews for this book in April of 2008 and finished near Christmas. At that time I hadn't done an interview since 1963, a span of forty-five years.

My last subject then was Lotte Lenya, who was tour-
ing with a show called *Brecht on Brecht*, a compilation of
material from her late husband, Kurt Weill, and Bertold
Brecht. Thinking of her playing in Berlin in the premieres
of *Three Penny Opera* and *Mahagonny* in the late twenties
and early thirties, with Nazi storm troopers rioting in the
aisles, I was in awe of her. I was twenty years old, and to
me she was one of History's witnesses.

She was in my mind as I returned to this genre
after all that time, during which I've written only fiction,
but I was looking for a different kind of witness, those
willing to reduce the focus to portrait mode and testify
about their own lives. I discovered--I either never knew
or had forgotten this--that the interviewer often has a peculiar ability to evoke a fair response. Something clearly
happens when the voice recorder comes out, when the
release form is produced saying that I may quote what
you say and use it in my book. It becomes *official*. People
sit up straighter, they look you in the eye, and they think
before they speak. It's almost like testifying during a trial.
The women are usually a little better dressed than if you
hadn't come. People are on the record. It's clearly an occasion, and they know they are going to have to live with
what they come up with even when they surprise themselves. Yet far from holding back, they often say remarkable and controversial things.

The unexpected power to evoke this response
didn't lead to arrogance on my part, far from it. I usually
began by saying I was writing this book because I knew
nothing whatever about the subject. This was convenient-
ly close to the truth, although it raised a few eyebrows and
seemed to confirm what many thought about some other

writers they'd read. It got me sympathy and made them inclined to help me out.

When I started I made few assumptions about how it would go. Most people seemed interested, even eager, to participate. Few declined. I was not surprised, but what did surprise me was the extreme range and variety of attitudes and experiences that emerged from these conversations. No two people were coming at San Miguel from the same direction. Was the place in some way a universal attraction? Did it have something for everyone, or was it merely everyone's panacea?

Was it the door to freedom or a way of forgetting, and was there any difference? Or was it a mirror in which people could finally see themselves? And would what they saw be what they really were or what they wanted to be? Was there anything behind that reflection beyond a middling Mexican town in the agricultural center? A hick town, as Carl Selph remarked with considerable fondness, but one with an overlay of gringo culture. If the periphery was vague, certain things emerged at the center.

There is a cultural gap too wide to bridge completely. Even those who have been here many years and have Mexican friends are still sensitive to the subtle distance between them and the natives. Relations can be cordial, generous, even affectionate and loving, but things usually stop just short of ultimate contact. There are expatriates here who will tell you that, although they have traveled the world, this is the most foreign place they have ever been.

One mitigating factor can be whether the Mexicans you're interested in connecting with have ever traveled, particularly to the United States. If their world is not circumscribed by the wedge of *barrio* they live in, if they have traveled farther than Celaya (forty kilometers away) in their lives, they are more likely to understand you better. The educational system here does not do much to provide a broad world view, and without something more, you may be simply incomprehensible to them in your values and manners, your attitudes toward family and religion, and your assumptions about life. Most Mexicans have watched some American TV, but it prepares them for real individual Americans about as much as Mexican TV prepares us for actual Mexicans.

Language is key. Almost everyone I talked to commented on it. Dave Richards said it as well as anyone. "Without speaking Spanish you're never going to learn about living here. Do whatever you have to do, but learn it. It's a nuanced language, a subtle language. That's your ticket into society."

Without it, as Cynthia Simmons pointed out, you can still live here, but you don't really penetrate far into the community. You can order in a restaurant, you can make a reservation in a bed and breakfast, but what happens when your water quits? What happens when your neighbor invites you to his daughter's fifteenth birthday celebration and you go and become the ultimate wallflower, silent and alone but smiling a lot?

One thread going through these narratives is that of sufficiency versus abundance. At times it is mentioned outright, at others only alluded to. America is proud of its abundance, but what is the human cost to participate? How much debt can we handle? Some people in these pages refer to it as a rat race, an old term, but one that still has meaning. How much more can we eat or wear? How much more space can we live in?

More importantly, what do we get for more work, beyond more and better stuff, and what opportunities to do other things do we lose in the process? People coming down here sometimes discover how much less they need, even though their dollars buy more. After paying a lot of money to move things down they find themselves giving much of it away.

There was a lot more politics in these conversations than I used. Most of it ended up on the cutting room floor, as they say in the movie business. Although I think Americans deserve better governance than we have gotten from either party in the last couple generations, I'm not much of a partisan myself, and coming out of an election year I felt the reader might have had enough of it already from other sources. I don't care for the shrillness of American political discourse from either side, and denying most of it a place here caused me no sleepless nights.

Although I listened for hints of it, these conversations yielded no sense of regret except from Jody Feagan and Dave Richards, the two who were leaving and didn't really want to. All the tradeoffs mentioned by others seemed to have been made with the satisfaction of getting the better part of the deal.

While there was a wide range of how closely people follow events in the States, even those who observe things in detail here also have the sense of doing so from a distance. This separation often leads to seeing America from a different viewpoint, from *outside*, where it is less important than it appears from within its own borders. Louise Gilliam referred to her Dallas suburb as a bubble. Maybe the bubble is bigger than Highland Park, Texas.

Maybe it's as large as an entire country, stretching from Atlantic to Pacific. It's possible that looking out through its filmy wall obscures or distorts everything beyond. The realization that there are other ways to be—for us as individuals—is more accessible from out here, from beyond the bubble. What those other ways might be is best left for each person to discover, and San Miguel de Allende might be one of the best places in which to make those discoveries.

Please visit the author's website:

www.sanmiguelallendebooks.com

JOHN SCHERBER

CPSIA information can be obtained at www.ICGtesting.com
Printed in the USA
LVOW06s1720120215

426801LV00001B/55/P

9 780983 258230